THE NOVELS OF GEORGE ELIOT

The Novels of George Eliot

Robert Liddell

Duckworth

First published in 1977 by
Gerald Duckworth & Co. Ltd.
The Old Piano Factory
43 Gloucester Crescent, London NW1

ISBN 0 7156 0992 0

Printed in Great Britain by
Unwin Brothers Limited
The Gresham Press, Old Woking, Surrey

To

H. S. Harvey

Contents

Abbreviations

George Eliot's works

SCL	*Scenes of Clerical Life*	*R*	*Romola*
AB	*Adam Bede*	*FH*	*Felix Holt*
MF	*The Mill on the Floss*	*M*	*Middlemarch*
SM	*Silas Marner*	*DD*	*Daniel Deronda*

Other books frequently cited

Critical Essays	Barbara Hardy (ed.), *Critical Essays on George Eliot* (London 1970)
Haight *Biography*	Gordon S. Haight, *George Eliot: a Biography* (Oxford 1968)
Haight *Letters*	Gordon S. Haight, *The George Eliot Letters*, 7 vols. (London 1954–6)

Note Double quotation marks are used for direct speech by characters in George Eliot's works, as well as for quotations within quotations.

I Introduction: 'Scenes of Clerical Life'

When I was invited to write a book on George Eliot I naturally felt great diffidence and hesitation; the subject has been so well treated and by so many people. After Lord David Cecil and Messrs Haight (that great George Eliot scholar), Harvey, Holloway and Leavis, and Mrs Bennet and Mrs Hardy and others, it seemed doubtful if there were anything left to do. Moreover, despite my intense admiration for *Middlemarch*, I have never felt a great personal sympathy for the Sibyl herself, and no author of comparable importance has more frequently irritated me by monstrosities of style. Nevertheless, in the vast territory of *Middlemarch* I thought there were still some gleanings to be made after the reapers. And elsewhere in the novels I have thought there were still observations to be recorded. Moreover it seemed to me that the time had perhaps come for a return to an old-fashioned and mainly aesthetic appreciation of her work.

Like (I suppose) most teachers of literature, I have constantly told students not 'to tell the story' when they have had to write about works of fiction. I have come to think this advice mistaken, for it would appear that to tell the story accurately is no common achievement. Even good and careful critics often make gross mistakes or reckless statements. I quote two such instances from critics of George Eliot (whom I forbear to name, as I admire them). One tells us that Silas Marner has been 'expelled from his little nonconformist community through a trick of blind chance'; but though it is by the drawing of lots that he is finally condemned for theft, the charge against him has been carefully and treacherously prepared. Another tells us that 'since the action of George Eliot's stories arises logically from the characters, those stories of fortune, coincidences, sudden inheritances, long-lost wills, which are the stock-in-trade of the ordinary Victorian novelist, are inevitably omitted'.

Nevertheless the legal problem of the Transome inheritance in *Felix Holt* is as elaborate as (and far more tiresome than) anything of the sort in Trollope's novels.

Is it, perhaps, a low esteem for the novel as an art, or is it merely the fact that each novel is long enough to be forgotten in detail if it has not frequently been re-read, that gives rise to such errors? In recent years even examination papers have not been free from them; candidates have, for example, been asked about such non-existent characters as 'Mrs Eliot' in Jane Austen's *Emma*. And only very self-important novelists will blame reviewers for not knowing their books.

It is the less surprising that false generalisations about novels should have been given authority by writers whom we usually read with respect. We have been told (for example) that there is as much cruelty at Thrushcross Grange as at Wuthering Heights; that many of Jane Austen's characters are cruel (though only Mrs Norris can be so described); that Jane Austen is often vulgar (though only a few utterances of Elizabeth Bennet's are in unintentional bad taste); that there is no vulgarity in Lawrence (and yet *Lady Chatterley's Lover* stinks of it).

The first step in criticism is to see clearly the artifact that we are criticising, and not another of our own fabrication. For this reason I shall carefully set out, for example, the complicated relationships of kindred and affinity which connect *Middlemarch*, and the details of the Transome inheritance in *Felix Holt*. This is not because I think there is any critical value in such an exercise, nor because I suppose that such pages can be agreeable reading: it is simply because it may be useful to other students to have the facts in front of them, for it could prevent them from making mistakes that might be of consequence.

More use will be made than has lately been the custom of the plot-character analysis: we know its inadequacies in the explanation of Shakespeare, but as it is a form of criticism derived from the study of nineteenth-century novels, it is as applicable to them as Aristotle's *Poetics* is to Greek tragedy.

Too much, perhaps, has been said about George Eliot's 'thought'. Though a highly intelligent and deeply reflective woman, she had no profound philosophy. She went beyond

Tennyson's 'honest doubt' into definite unbelief. Her conversation with F. W. H. Myers in the Fellows' Garden of Trinity College, Cambridge, is often quoted. 'She, stirred somewhat beyond her wont, and taking as her text the three words which have been used so often as the inspiring trumpet-call of men — the words, *God, Immortality, Duty* — pronounced with terrible earnestness, how inconceivable was the *first*, how unbelievable the *second*, and yet how peremptory and absolute the *third*.'[1]

It is not here worthwhile to discriminate between the exact positions held by Matthew Arnold, George Eliot and other Victorian rationalists about Christianity. They were in favour of it, and they did not believe in it. T. S. Eliot, among others, has pointed out the anti-intellectual consequences of such a position, and it may be enquired, if only an ethical system were wanted, what need they had of the Gospels.

For Matthew Arnold, religion is 'not simply morality, but *morality touched by emotion*'. He says: 'The *Guardian* proclaims "the miracle of the incarnation" to be the "fundamental truth" for Christians. How strange that on me should devolve the office of instructing the *Guardian* that the fundamental thing for Christians is not the Incarnation but the Imitation of Christ!' Eliot, citing this passage, well points out the muddle arising from comparison of a ' "fundamental truth" in theology, and a "fundamental thing" in his own loose jargon'. He wonders whether 'Arnold's own "imitation" is even a good piece of mimicry'.[2] One might go further and say that those who do not believe in the Incarnation can only have aesthetic reasons for the imitation of Christ rather than that of some other moral teacher, such as Socrates.

It is a strange thing that in that age men who were openly unorthodox, and ready to suffer for it, were yet unwilling to say that they were without religion. We know that many people are debarred from this or that vital experience – so far debarred that they cannot even conceive what it is. Thus the tone-deaf are debarred from music and the blind from the plastic arts and from natural scenery. We know that if such people are brave and intelligent there is enough left to them from which a full and satisfying life can be made. We are

[1] cit. *Biography*, p. 464.
[2] Essay on *Arnold and Pater*.

justifiably irritated if a tone-deaf person, for example, tells us that architecture is 'his music'. It is not. 'Everything is what it is and not another thing.' You may help yourself more lavishly to potatoes if you cannot eat meat, but you are not to say that potatoes are 'your' meat. Only religion is religion, and there is no substitute for it. This is not to say that many people have not led admirable lives and have not been eminent ethical teachers without it. The chief mischief that unbelief can do to a writer is to expose him to foolish and false beliefs (like those of D. H. Lawrence), or to the sloppy sentimentality that disfigures otherwise beautiful work by E. M. Forster. The Jews, when they forsook Jehovah, did not forsake him for atheism, but went 'whoring after strange gods'. It is infinitely to the credit of George Eliot that she did not do anything of the sort.

It would surely be better to confine such words as *religion, sacred, divine, holy* and the like – as also *irreverent, blasphemy, sacrilege* – to subjects connected with a Deity conceived of as a Being, numinous, and existing objectively outside human minds. These words can only properly be used by Theists or Deists, of whatever persuasion, and are degraded to sentimentality when used by unbelievers. It must be supposed that they intend metaphor or analogy when they speak, for example, of a 'reverent attitude to life', where such an adjective as 'serious' or 'responsible' would better fit their meaning than the more emotive word. George Eliot is not free from these confusions.

She started her career as a writer of fiction under the influence of the *Essence of Christianity* by Ludwig Feuerbach, which she had lately translated. This essence they both held to be purely humanistic. Such an attitude to Christianity is no doubt still shared by many humanists. It consists in a 'reverence' (which could be better expressed as a 'deep and peculiar respect') for the purely human part of the Gospel story, a love for Christ, considered as a human being, and for his ethical teaching. The redemption and the mystery of the Passion thus become no more than a beautiful and edifying myth. Such an attitude is akin to that of Renan, whose 'charmant docteur' is made so attractive that (contrary to the author's intention) he has converted many readers to the Christian church. At the other end of the scale is a great deal of mawkish or hearty writing about 'Jesus of Nazareth', as distinguished from Christ. Of this the most distressing example is probably Ezra Pound's *Ballad of the Goodly Fere.*

In the age in which she lived, it is hard to imagine George Eliot holding a very different intellectual position; though it might have been better for her work if she had got over her nostalgia for Christianity, and had accepted a position nearer to that of Samuel Butler. In an age of faith – in the *grand siècle* – one can imagine her as a disciple of Port Royal.

As things were, her early education in the Church of England was overlaid by the influence of nonconformist friends, and she had acquired the nonconformist conscience before she became a free-thinker. C. S. Lewis has written of the unhappy plight of agnostics whose ancestors had been Puritans: 'The Puritan conscience works on without Puritan theology – like millstones grinding nothing, like digestive juices working on an empty stomach and producing ulcers.' Her Puritanism had become a habit of mind, without the faith that once gave it warmth. The temples of Apollo are lovely even in ruins – the nonconformist chapel, when faith in and love for God are gone, has only a shadow to cast.

Lord David Cecil had reason on his side when he wrote: 'The enlightened person of today must forget his dislike of Puritanism when he reads George Eliot.'[3] This made Dr Leavis very (and most unnecessarily) angry. Lord David on another page, and in praise of George Eliot, says: 'Her standards of right and wrong were the Puritan standards. She admired truthfulness and chastity and industry and self-restraint, she disapproved of loose-living and recklessness and deceit and self-indulgence . . .' Dr Leavis leaps on this passage, and says: 'I had better confess that I differ (apparently) from Lord David Cecil in sharing these beliefs, admirations and disapprovals . . . And they seem to me favourable to the production of great literature.'

So they must seem to everyone. Matthew Arnold rightly censures 'men of culture' who have often been without the virtues as well as the faults of the Puritan; it has been one of their dangers that they so felt the Puritan's faults that they

[3] *Early Victorian Novelists*, ch. 8.

too much neglected the practice of his virtues.' Nevertheless 'their ideal of beauty, of sweetness and light . . . remains the true ideal of perfection still; just as the Puritan's ideal of perfection remains narrow and inadequate . . .'[4]

Dr Leavis, however, seems to think he has floored his adversary by this miserable sophism, of a kind which (according to Port Royal) 'un homme de bien et sincère doit éviter sur toutes choses'.[5] If 'the enlightened person of today' dislikes Puritanism, it is in spite of, not because of its virtues.

It is surprising that so great a critic as Dr Leavis has permitted this passage to be reprinted. He professes to admire truthfulness and self-restraint, and to disapprove of deceit and recklessness and self-indulgence; yet here he is indulging in dishonest controversy and reckless language, and not at all restraining his temper – though there was nothing to be cross about. Moreover the liberal arts are supposed to soften our manners, and criticism ought to be a part of polite letters. While 'intemperance in talk' (as Bishop Wilson said) 'makes a dreadful havoc in the heart'.

Puritans have not the monopoly of truthfulness and chastity and industry and self-restraint; nor are these the only virtues. There are also what may be called the Cavalier virtues, of honour, courtesy and generosity; these are the virtues of a gentleman and should be those of a scholar.

It may be well to attempt a sympathetic and (I hope) non-controversial definition of Puritanism. It will generally be found (at all events in the Western world) that every religion or philosophy of life that has any claim to respect has always maintained two moral standards. There is the moral law, which is binding on everyone, and there are the counsels of perfection which are for the chosen few who are called to be perfect here on earth – such are the Guardians of Plato's

---

[4] *Culture and Anarchy*, ch. 1.

[5] On *Ignoratio Elenchi*. 'C'est un vice très ordinaire dans les contestations des hommes. On dispute avec chaleur, et souvent on ne s'entend pas l'un l'autre. La passion ou la mauvaise foi fait qu'on attribue à son adversaire ce qui est éloigné de son sentiment, pour le combattre avec plus d'avantage, ou qu'on lui impute les consequences qu'on s'imagine pouvoir tirer de sa doctrine, quoiqu'il les désavoue et qu'il les nie. Tout cela peut se rapporter à cette première espèce de sophisme qu'un homme de bien et sincère doit éviter sur toutes choses.' *Logique de Port Royal*, III, xix. 1.

Republic, and monks, who divest themselves of all earthly ties in order to devote themselves to the service of God. The fault of the Puritan is that too often he fails to recognise the duality of these standards, and tries unremittingly to apply the higher standard – especially to the conduct of other people. His merit is that he keeps us continually aware of the higher standard, as we ought to be. It will be seen later how far less narrow George Eliot's moral sympathies were than those of Puritanism, although its influence on her cannot be denied.

When we come to examine what Puritanism means in a modern English setting we must dismiss some of the grander ideas that the word may produce in our minds – we must forget such good and beautiful things as the prose style of Plato or of Pascal, as the noble frugality of life in Stoic households under the Roman republic, or the pure lines of a great Cistercian church in England or Northern France. We are in a very different world.

The first thing about English Puritanism is its stifling narrowness and provinciality. This is the result of a double schism. When the national Church broke away from the rest of the Western Church it retained a tradition and claims to historicity which still connected it with Europe – with the Greco-Roman world and the undivided church of the patristic age. One may go one step further: men reared in the tradition and civilised decorum of the National Church, but who have broken from it, have nevertheless retained its gifts into after life. Milton was a son of Anglican Cambridge, and John Wesley a son of Anglican Oxford. It is in the second generation of the Puritan schism that the rot starts and, as Matthew Arnold wrote: 'Puritanism produces men of national mark no more.'[6]

For now we are faced with something to which a less distinguished name should be given – we are now concerned not so much with Puritanism as with dissent or Protestant nonconformity. It is a lamentable thing that some people in our time should have tried to exalt the nonconformist chapel above the parish church as a symbol of English cultural life.

There is another Humanism (that defined by T. S. Eliot) broader than that of Feuerbach or George Eliot, and not excluding Theism, Christianity, Judaism and (possibly) other

[6] *Culture and Anarchy*, preface.

religions than those of the 'Book'. 'Humanism', wrote Eliot, 'can have no positive theories about philosophy or theology. All that it can ask, in the most tolerant spirit, is: Is this philosophy or religion civilised or not?' Again: 'It is not the business of Humanism to refute anything.. Its business is to persuade, according to its unformulable axioms of culture and good sense . . . it operates by taste, by sensibility trained by culture. It is critical rather than constructive.'[7]

Let us enquire, then, in a tolerant spirit, whether non-conformity is civilised or not; and, as Aristotle recommends, let us take as our starting-point the opinions of ordinary people and the cultivated.

What do ordinary people think? They will tell you emphatically that no nonconformist is a gentleman. So firmly and universally is this believed that a successful tradesman who has raised his family in the world and begins to have aspirations towards gentility will (like Bulstrode in *Middlemarch*) forsake the nonconformist chapel for the established church. Kenneth Kirk, formerly bishop of Oxford, concealed through life from his son that he had been brought up as a Methodist.[8] This indicates that nonconformists themselves do not believe nonconformity to be civilised, for the concept 'gentleman' includes some vague notion of civilisation.

Let us go higher, to the opinions of men in public life. How often when asked why they could not make the English Sunday a little less depressing, the licensing laws more reasonable, and those about sexual offences more humane – why, in short, they could not make England more like any other progressive European country – have they not replied: 'We have to think of the nonconformist vote'?

Let us go higher still, to the two greatest English creative writers, to Shakespeare and Dickens. For Dickens the non-conformist is Stiggins or Chadband, for Shakespeare the Puritan is Malvolio. Sir Toby's reply to him (sot though Toby is) is the answer of Shakespeare and indeed of the English people to Puritanism: 'Dost thou think that because thou art virtuous there shall be no more cakes and ale?'

In George Eliot's early books Puritanism is most evident:

[7] *Second Thoughts on Humanism.*
[8] Rose Macaulay, *Last Letters to a Friend* (London 1962), pp. 264–5.

in the Clerical Scenes Amos Barton is said to be 'half a dissenter' and Edgar Tryan is on the extreme outside edge of Evangelicalism. Dissent is the form taken by such intellectual life as there is in the countryside of *Adam Bede*, and in the Lantern Yard of *Silas Marner*.

The author regrets that to some of her readers 'Methodism may mean nothing more than low-pitched gables up dingy streets, sleek grocers, sponging preachers and hypocritical jargon – elements which are regarded as an exhaustive analysis of Methodism in many fashionable quarters'.[9] This she says, is a pity, for there are excellent people among them, well deserving our sympathy. No doubt; but the 'low-pitched gables, sleek grocers, sponging preachers and hypocritical jargon' also existed. It is harder for an author to create sympathy for his characters if they are situated in so unattractive a world; and it is no merit in him as an artist to have placed himself under such a disadvantage. It is true that some reviewers, and even the Nobel committee, have been known to reward authors for extending the background of fiction, but it may be doubted if this is an achievement worthy of critical approval.

Puritanism had two other unfortunate effects on George Eliot. To it must be attributed her didacticism. Dr Leavis apologises for this by pointing out how didactic Jane Austen can be, and how improving a book is *Emma*. There is, however, a great difference. Jane Austen, a purer artist, did not write in order to edify. Her object was to create work 'in which the most thorough knowledge of human nature, the happiest delineation of its varieties, the liveliest effusions of wit and humour are conveyed to the world in the best chosen language'. Anything so conveyed to the world by such a woman must contain edification as well as beauty – another by-product of the work and not to be deliberately aimed at.[10] George Eliot, on the other hand, sometimes harps, sometimes underlines the

[9] *AB*, ch. 5. In the phrase 'fashionable quarters' one may hear something of that envy and sense of social inferiority so marked in D. H. Lawrence.

[10] 'I do not deny that art may be affirmed to serve ends beyond itself; but art is not required to be aware of those ends, and indeed performs its function, whatever that may be according to various theories of value, much better in indifference to them.' T. S. Eliot, *The Function of Criticism*.

moral lesson, sometimes tries to create a moral conflict where there is none.

Another defect arising from the same cause, is her feeling that there are some subjects on which jests may not be made – a very unEnglish feeling. Of course a jest may be ill-timed or in bad taste, whatever its subject, but no subject is in itself sacrosanct. Few people, for instance, are 'an exception to the rule that enthusiasm for religious subjects is coupled with a tendency to pleasantry upon them'.[11] When one of the witnesses in the defence of Lady Chatterley quoted Archbishop William Temple as saying that Christians did not make jokes about sex because it was 'sacred' (and one may well ask why?) it is amazing that no one pointed out that Archbishop William Temple had been talking through his mitre, and had chosen to forget such Christians as Shakespeare, Chaucer and Dryden. Inhibition about humour may well be a part of the evil heritage of Puritanism. In the supremely humourless Lawrence it hardly mattered, but it may have prevented George Eliot from an adequate exploitation of her rich humorous vein – it may have turned her aside into the dreadful sesquipedalian humour which she so much affects, which could offend no one by its subject matter.

George Eliot's most interesting examination of ethical problems owes nothing to Puritanism, and is even contrary to its spirit. More than any other great novelist of her time she appreciated Casuistry, and also understood that people can become better as the result of their faults.

The dictionary definition of Casuistry is: 'that part of Ethics which resolves cases of conscience, applying the general rules of religion and morality to particular instances which disclose special circumstances, or conflicting duties.' It is that science by which the stern edicts of the moral law – practised literally by the chosen few – are adapted to weaker vessels. Some of George Eliot's characters are allowed to descend from the heights, to a lower but honourable place. We cannot think quite so highly of Dinah Morris when she is the Rev. Mrs Adam Bede – celibacy of what may be called the female clergy is an aesthetic necessity. Dorothea also climbs down

[11] I. Compton-Burnett, *Dolores*.

from her pedestal when she marries Ladislaw. Felix Holt gives up some of his independence to settle down cosily with Esther and a small income. George Eliot is too much identified with Maggie to allow her to come down to a lower position, and can do nothing but drown her.

She was, of course, completely aware of what she was doing. The *locus classicus* occurs when Dr Kenn is thinking over Maggie's plight:

'The great problem of the shifting relation between passion and duty is clear to no man who is capable of apprehending it: the question whether the moment has come in which a man has fallen below the possibility of a renunciation that will carry any efficacy, and must accept the sway of a passion against which he had struggled as a trespass, is one for which we have no master-key that will fit all cases. The casuists have become a byeword of reproach; but their perverted spirit of minute discrimination was the shadow of a truth to which eyes and hearts are too often fatally sealed – the truth that moral judgments must remain false and hollow, unless they are checked and enlightened by a perpetual reference to the special circumstances that mark the individual lot.'[12]

No doubt her enthusiasm for the *Pensées* of Pascal had led George Eliot to read his *Provinciales*, and from that delightful (and wicked) book, a great favourite with Gibbon, she had learned to see the necessity of casuistry behind the immoral quibbling of some of the casuists.

Philip Debarry, always presented as a man of the highest integrity, says: "In special cases we have to do with special conditions. You know I defend the casuists."[13] And Felix Holt says: "The old Catholics are right, with their higher rule and their lower. Some are called to subject themselves to a harder discipline, and renounce things voluntarily which are lawful for others."[14] Much of Dorothea Brooke's thought is concerned with such renunciations.

George Eliot has always been famous for her mastery of the theme of temptation: I cannot recollect who said that Satan had far more to learn from her than from Flaubert. The temptations of Arthur Donnithorne, of Maggie, of Bulstrode

---

[12] *MF*, vii, ii.   [13] *FH*, ch. 23.   [14] ibid. ch. 27.

and of Gwendolen Harleth are among the strongest scenes that
she ever wrote.

Her notion of the virtue that can be the consequence of sin
is not the sentimental notion:

> that men may rise on stepping-stones
> Of their dead selves to higher things.

And it cannot, of course, be the doctrine of the Church:
O felix culpa! – rendered by Dame Julian and T. S. Eliot as
'sin is behovely'. Nevertheless, with a different meaning, she
might have said that sin was 'behovely' – not only because
reaction from it can be nobly virtuous, but because it springs
from a spiritual energy, which may be good. Maggie says to her
brother, Tom; "I know I have been wrong – often, continually.
But yet, sometimes when I've done wrong, it is because I have
feelings that you would be the better for, if you had them."[15]

Bulstrode, for all his messy religion, and indeed because of it,
is yet in many ways a better man than Vincy, his brother-in-
law. Arthur Donnithorne's good qualities are brought out even
in his unsuccessful struggle against temptation; and after his
sin, and the severe penance he does for it, he will be a larger
person. The whole life of Gwendolen Harleth in *Daniel Deronda*
(it is suggested) is the sentimental education of a saint.

The ultimate sanctity of Gwendolen, to which Deronda points
her, is wisely not given. George Eliot's lack of religious
certainty made her uncertain when she tried to get inside
religious characters (Dorothea Brooke, Maggie Tulliver,
Dino in *Romola*). They had strayed beyond her very considerable range.

Too much has been said about George Eliot as a social
thinker: happily she was no such thing, and therefore she has
not become unreadable like Charles Reade or Kingsley. Her
best novels are set in time past; of time present she is an acute
observer, but her object is to be the '*aesthetic*' not the 'doctrinal
teacher' aiming only at 'the rousing of the nobler emotions
which make mankind desire the social right'.[16] She is well
aware that 'there is no private life which has not been determined by a wider public life;'[17] but the determination is not

---

[15] *MF*, vv.   [16] Haight *Letters*, VII, p. 44.   [17] *FH*, ch. 3.

absolute, and the determining public life need not be very wide, and can (as in *Middlemarch*) be parochial. The lives of her characters are never so violently altered by affairs so public as are those in Thackeray's *Vanity Fair* by the Hundred Days.

In fact, George Eliot had little faith in politics. Moreover she certainly shared Matthew Arnold's horror of mob violence. It is hardly fair to say that 'she finds it easier to excuse or ignore the use of violence if it is associated with the defence of an established order'.[18] I think it should rather be said that she always condemned and hated violence (which is indiscriminate) but did not unreservedly condemn force, as no one can who accepts the protection of the law. Force, after all, can only be applied by established order, and may be just. The distinction between Force and Violence is surely a moral necessity; when it is neglected we see such idiocy as a mawkish sympathy for 'political' offenders (who have, perhaps, expressed their political opinions in such unattractive ways as planting bombs about) and a greater horror at the capital punishment of murderers than at their crimes.

George Eliot, to her great credit, refused to contribute to the Mazzini fund, explaining that 'though she would gladly give for Mazzini's personal use, she feared this fund would ultimately be used to promote conspiracy, and perhaps acts "more unsocial in their character than the very wrong they are expected to extinguish" '[19] – unfortunately her fears were only too well founded.

Of the proposed series of Clerical Scenes G. H. Lewes wrote to the publisher John Blackwood: 'It will consist of tales and sketches illustrative of the actual life of our clergy about a quarter of a century ago, but solely in its *human* and not at all in its *theological* aspect; the object being to do what has never yet been done in our Literature, for we have had abundant religious stories polemical and doctrinal, but since the 'Vicar' and Miss Austen, no series representing the clergy like any other class with the humours, sorrows and troubles of other men.'[20]

[18] Arnold Kettle, in *Critical Essays*, p. 114.
[19] Haight *Biography*, p. 395.   [20] Haight *Biography*, I, p. 274.

This is self-contradictory; if Lewes meant to say that there was an object of doing something in our Literature that had not been done by Goldsmith even, or Jane Austen, he has been very awkward in saying so.

'Why', ask recent critics,[21] 'should George Eliot have decided to begin her writing with scenes of *clerical* life, if not to give herself the best focus for discussing the *essence* of Christianity?'

There might be other reasons, not least, the example of Goldsmith's *Vicar of Wakefield*. Moreover the central position of the clergy among all classes in country life provides an excellent focus for observing them. It may be doubted whether the Clerical Scenes were so suitable a background for the discussion of religious interests.

George Eliot was indeed, as the same critics demonstrate, intellectually dominated by Feuerbach at this time, and believed with him that the 'essence' of Christianity was purely humanistic. It is true that the goodness of her clergy (and most of them are good) is hardly ever to be referred to a supernatural motive – Tryan is an exception, and even Tryan repents more bitterly for his sin against a human being than for his sin against God. Nevertheless, all of them are believers in English Protestantism of one kind or another. The agnostic clergyman (such as Oscar Jekyll in Ivy Compton-Burnett's novel *A House and Its Head*) never makes an appearance; indeed he would be something of an anachronism at the time when the Scenes are situated.

Her clergy speak the language of their profession. Amos Barton 'talked of Israel and its sins, of chosen vessels, of the Paschal lamb, of blood as a medium of reconciliation'. He had been 'University-taught' – but at his University he had not acquired perfect accuracy in English orthography and syntax, and he was without 'flexible imagination' or 'adroit tongue'. He could not even bring the horrors of Hell home to the inmates of the pauper institution.

Maynard Gilfil, more spiritually-minded, is able to speak to the soul of Caterina: "God saw your whole heart; He knows you would never harm a living thing. He watches over His

[21] Derek and Sybil Oldfield in *Critical Essays*, p. 2.

children, and will not let them do things they would pray with their whole hearts not to do. It was the thought of a moment, and He forgives you." He is of course speaking in character, as one believer to another.

Edgar Tryan, in 'Janet's Repentance', is continually using words such as "the Saviour", "Heaven" and "divine strength". It is hardly surprising that Crabb Robinson[22] found it hypocritical and offensive: 'It is so very Evangelical in its tone that it is quite unpleasant thinking of it as the writing of Miss Evans' – that is of a notorious 'fallen woman' and freethinker. George Eliot ran a risk of being misinterpreted in this way by her choice of characters, and one cannot be sure that it was worth her while. Amos Barton, indeed, is so unattractive, that there can be no danger of his being taken for the author's mouthpiece; Maynard Gilfil's love-story has little to do with his clerical life; but Edgar Tryan is as unthinkable without religious ardour as Dinah Morris would be.

George Eliot's method invites real confusion when she departs from dialogue, and writes such a passage as this from 'Amos Barton': 'O the anguish of that thought that we can never atone to our dead for the stinted affection we gave them, for the light answers we returned to their plaints or their pleadings, or the little reverence we showed to that sacred human soul that lived so close to us, and was the divinest thing God had given us to know.' Are these the thoughts of Amos, better expressed than the poor creature could himself have expressed them? Or are they the comments of the narrator, who makes a casual appearance from time to time (and must be considered later)? Or are they the words of the author, and what can she mean by 'reverence', 'sacred', 'God' or 'divinest'? If George Eliot had really wished to make her clergy – supporters of a doctrinal and traditional Christianity – a focus for examining the humanistic sub-Christianity of Feuerbach, one cannot think that she chose wisely, for confusion of this kind is almost inevitable. But it is not likely that this was her purpose. She could not have said (with Miss Pratt in 'Janet's Repentance'), "I have ever considered fiction a suitable form for conveying moral and religious instruction." On the

contrary, when she was still a believer, she had written:
'Religious novels are more hateful to me than merely worldly
ones... The weapons of Christian warfare were never sharpened
at the forge of romance.'[23] There is no reason to suppose that
she thought that forge more propitious to the blunt instruments
of 'essential' Christianity.

It may be an effect of her Puritanism that in her early work
George Eliot deliberately chose drab subjects, just as Methodists chose plain bonnets. Her object was, at this time, to
extend the range of human sympathy, and it may be doubted if
she realised the limits of fiction as a power towards this end,
or understood that it could have no power towards any end
without art. A long passage from *Adam Bede* must be quoted at
this point, to show her confusion of thought.

'All honour and reverence to the divine beauty of form!
Let us cultivate it to the utmost... But let us love that other
beauty, too, which lies in no secret of proportion, but in the
secret of deep human sympathy. Paint us an angel, if you can,
with a floating violet robe, and a face paled by the celestial
light . . . but do not impress on us any aesthetic rules which
shall banish from the region of Art those old women scraping
carrots with their work-worn hands... In this world there are
so many of these common, coarse people, who have no
picturesque, sentimental wretchedness! It is so needful we
should remember their existence, else we may happen to leave
them quite out of our religion and philosophy, and frame
lofty theories which only fit a world of extremes. Therefore
let Art always remind us of them: therefore let us always have
men ready to give the loving pains of a life to the faithful
reproducing of commonplace things, and delight in showing
how kindly the light of heaven falls on them.'[24]

In the same chapter she had praised Dutch paintings
'which many lofty-minded people despise' for their truthfulness. 'I find a source of delicious sympathy in these faithful
pictures of a monotonous homely existence, which has been the
fate of so many more among my fellow-mortals than a life of
pomp or of absolute indigence, of tragic suffering, or of world-
stirring actions. I turn without shrinking from cloudborne

[23] Haight *Biography*, I, pp. 22–3.
[24] *AB*, ch. 17.

angels, from prophets, sibyls and heroic warriors, to an old woman bending over her flowerpot, or eating her solitary dinner, while the noon-day light, softened perhaps by a screen of leaves, falls on her mob-cap, and just touches the rim of her spinning-wheel, and her stone jug, and all those cheap, common things which are the necessities of life to her.'

The divine light that a great Dutch painter lets fall on an old woman watering a flower-pot will indeed make her more significant than a cloud-borne angel or a heroic warrior on whom no such light falls. But the painter's Art might make the warrior equally significant. George Eliot passes almost insensibly from the truthful assertion that one subject is as good as another in Art, to expressing a preference for 'the faithful representing of commonplace things'. It is more useful, no doubt, that we should have sympathy for the ordinary people who surround us in life, than for heroes, prophets and 'picturesque lazzaroni', with whom we may reasonably hope to have nothing to do. It is, however, no business of Art intentionally to create this sympathy by direct representation.

Ruskin had exhibited the same nineteenth-century Philistinism when he wrote of Murillo's beggars: 'Do you feel moved with any charity towards children as you look at them? Are we the least likely to take an interest in ragged schools, or to help the next pauper child that comes in our way, because the painter has shown us a cunning beggar feeding greedily?'[25] On this passage Cavafy rightly commented: 'What is the meaning of the questions? What have they to do with Art? Is it the task of Art to answer such questions?'[26]

George Eliot appears to accept (as any artist must) the principle of selection, but unhappily her selection is – at this time of her life – to be made with utilitarian aims. She forgets the vital reason for selection in Art, to avoid dullness and the banal. She also forgets the different functions of the different arts: because Painting can present 'faithful pictures of a monotonous homely existence' without boring us, it does not follow that Fiction can.

'Depend upon it,' she wrote, 'you would gain unspeakably if you would learn with me to see some of the poetry and the

[25] *Stones of Venice*, II, vi, §60.
[26] Robert Liddell, *Cavafy* (London 1974), p. 117.

pathos, the tragedy and the comedy, lying in the experience of a human soul that looks out through dull grey eyes, and that speaks in a voice of quite ordinary tones.'[27] She does not tell us what we should gain, and it is perhaps legitimate to wonder if this is not one of the occasions when she did not quite know what she was saying. It is certainly legitimate to object that, though pathos and comedy are to be found in Amos Barton's experience, it lacks poetry or tragedy.

Poetry, of course, would depend on George Eliot, not upon her hero: Crabbe might have done something for him, but she was no poet. Barton's 'dull grey eyes' and his 'quite ordinary tones' do not repel us, for we neither see them nor hear them. What repels us is his lack of grammar and sympathy, and his silliness. Like the people of Shepperton we do come to feel for him in his *Sad Fortunes*, but it is a mistake to call them tragic. Not everything that is sad is tragic – no accident can be, for all the misery that it may cause. No Greek tragedy depends upon accident, and one may call *Romeo and Juliet* a comedy that ends unhappily. A tragedy can only come out of the characters of the people in it, and they must be large enough for tragedy. Nothing that happens to Amos Barton can be more than pathetic, though the pathos is genuine. In literature drab misery and monotony are apt to be merely drab and monotonous. It is not until the advent of the cinema (perhaps not before the post-war Italian film) that an art has been found to represent this too common a part of human experience truthfully, swiftly enough to retain interest, and yet capable of drawing beauty from it.

'Mr Gilfil's Love-Story' is far less satisfactory. Mr Gilfil is presented in an apologetic way, but is a perfectly amiable old man for whom no apology is needed. He was fond of his pipe and gin-and-water, but his 'potations of gin-and-water were quite moderate'. If he were anxious to save money to leave to his nephew 'the propensity showed itself rather in the parsimony of his personal habits, than in withholding help from the needy'. The sentimental love-story with Caterina and its melodramatic climax do nothing to explain him – the events might have happened to an entirely different person, and in

---

[27] 'Amos Barton', v.

no way does he seem to have been moulded by them. There is even a loose end in the story: his patron Sir Christopher always meant to give him the Cheverel living of Cumbermoor, and yet we find him ending his days at Shepperton.

'Janet's Repentance' is the most interesting of the *Scenes*. Janet Dempster, married to a brutal and drunken lawyer, herself takes to drink. Nevertheless she is always very charitable to the poor, and at the bedside of a consumptive girl she meets the Evangelical clergyman, Edgar Tryan, at whom she has been accustomed to jeer. She is greatly moved when she overhears him say: "Pray for me, Sally, that I may have strength too when the hour of great suffering comes. It is one of my worst weaknesses to shrink from bodily pain, and I think the time is perhaps not far off when I shall have to bear what you are bearing."

Sympathy with his 'sad fortunes' had brought his parishioners round to Amos Barton. 'The most brilliant deed of virtue could not have inclined Janet's good-will towards Mr Tryan as much as this fellowship in suffering'. When Dempster flings her out of the house in a rage, she takes refuge with a woman friend, and sends to Tryan for comfort. She goes back to nurse her husband in a fatal illness, and is supported by Tryan in her victorious effort to overcome her temptation. It is a weak point in her story that we never see Janet do anything that needs repentance, though once she is sorely tempted – but George Eliot probably shrank from depicting a drunken woman, and drunkenness is seldom successful in literature unless it is comic. It is a further weak point that Tryan is given a sin in the past to expiate – the seduction of a young girl when he was an undergraduate – and that so poor a story is made of this quite unnecessary sin. The moral rehabilitation of Janet and the goodness of Tryan are true and moving, though Janet has at times the tiresome sprightliness that we shall later find in Mary Garth.

It was suitable to George Eliot's function as 'the *aesthetic* not doctrinal teacher' that her stories should be placed in the past. She could thus be detached from the interests of the immediate present, whose confusion is often fatal to the artist. Part of the failure of *Daniel Deronda* is due to her abandonment of this practice, and it is now ironical to think that his Zionism was intended as a step towards world peace. It was a breach of her own excellent resolution against the 'prescribing of special measures, concerning which the artistic mind, however strongly moved by social sympathy, is often not the best judge'.[28] It is not, and George Eliot was wiser in her generation than many writers of today who, out of enthusiasm, or for self-advertisement, are only too ready to give their names to protests about subjects on which they have no special infor-mation, and no claim to authority.

Moreover she liked the English past, and her imagination moved freely in it, as did that of Dickens. 'Mine', she wrote, 'is not a well-regulated mind: it has an occasional tenderness for old abuses; it lingers with a certain fondness over the days of nasal clerks and top-booted parsons, and has a sigh for the departed shades of vulgar errors.'[29] A love for 'things counter, original, spare, strange' is a characteristic of most artists, and must cause them many a backward look. A country-woman like George Eliot had grown up among farmers, for whom the golden age had been that of the Napoleonic wars and dear corn, and for whom 'all guarantees of human advancement' did little in comparison.

Great novels are seldom 'contemporary', and novelists who strive for up-to-dateness often achieve out-of-dateness while their work is still in proof. It was as natural for George Eliot to situate her works in the past as for Dickens to revert to the coaching age, and Thackeray to the age of Waterloo, or for Proust or Joyce (despite the Great War in between) to go back to the Dreyfus trial, or to a day in Dublin more than a decade before. A writer seldom writes about the future until his best powers are exhausted.

Some of George Eliot's scenes could be expressed in the pluperfect; Amos was at Shepperton 'five-and-twenty years ago', but he did not go there 'until long after Mr Gilfil had departed this life'; and the love-story of Mr Gilfil's youth belonged to a yet remoter past. There are also flashes forward into the time of writing. 'More than a quarter of a century has slipped by since then, and in the interval Milby has advanced at as rapid a pace as other market-towns in Her Majesty's

[28] Haight *Biography*, VII, p. 44.
[29] 'Amos Barton', I.

dominions. By this time it has a handsome railway station, where the drowsy London traveller may look out by the brilliant gas-light and see perfectly sober papas and husbands alighting with their leather bags after transacting their day's business at the county town'.[30] These criss-cross time references strengthen the historicity of the background, and the Milby of Tryan's day is all the more real for being lit up by the brilliant gas-light of the eighteen-fifties.

It was a less successful device to introduce a narrator, who sometimes appears in the first person and remembers his childhood. He is a boy, and perhaps we may call him 'George Eliot'. There seems to be another less clearly defined narrator who also says 'I', but makes only general statements; she (for she seems feminine) may be called Marian Evans. 'George' had to be coaxed into good behaviour at Shepperton church by bread and butter smuggled into 'the sacred edifice' by his nurse. He was also present at the confirmation at Milby. It is interesting that he went home and made his little sister cry by imitating the sonorous tones of one of the clergy. Perhaps 'George' had something of Isaac Evans in him. He reappears in *Adam Bede* to talk to Adam as an old man.

Very occasionally, when the author remembers the existence of 'George', there is an attempt at masculinity, but one can feel no surprise that from the first readers had no doubt that the *Scenes* were written by a woman.

The sentimental treatment of the heroines will be largely corrected in the later novels. Caterina, the 'little singing-bird', the 'humming-bird', the 'little southern bird', fortunately makes no further appearance: the scales are somewhat weighted against Hetty in *Adam Bede*, and the other 'victim' (if so she may be called), Molly in *Silas Marner*, is an opium addict. Milly Barton, 'a large, fair, gentle Madonna', is something of a foretaste of Dorothea Brooke in *Middlemarch* and shares Dorothea's unheroic trait of short-sight – but she has no other of Dorothea's shortcomings, and is unbelievably perfect. She does, however, make a sensible end. As Leslie Stephen observed: 'We are never crossed by the thought which disturbs so many death-beds in fiction that she is somehow

[30] *JR*, 2.

conscious of an audience applauding her excellence in the part.'

About motherhood George Eliot (who avoided it for herself) is not only sentimental but quite unreal. 'A mother dreads no memories', she says of Caterina, '– those shadows have all melted away in the dawn of a baby's smile.' It is suggested that the 'mighty force of motherhood' might have kept Janet from the bottle; she must, however, have been thankful that there were no children in the Dempster household, which was no place for them.

George Eliot's children are always badly done: readers who dislike her dialect and prefer fictional characters to talk pure English may (if they think it worth while) defend themselves from the charge of snobbery by including her baby-talk in their censure. We are told that George Eliot was loved by her sister Chrissy's children, but it is difficult to imagine her talking to a child. Babies are to her as genderless as cats are to people who do not like cats; we shall never know if Hetty or Caterina had a boy or a girl.

It is the humour in the *Scenes*, whether in dialogue or summary, that gives the best promise of what is to come.

Lady Assher in 'Mr Gilfil's Love-Story' has the accents of Jane Austen's Lady Catherine de Bourgh, from whom she may probably be derived. She is discussing burial in wool. "Of course you must have a woolen dress, because it is the law, you know, but that need hinder no one from putting linen underneath. I always used to say, 'If Sir John died tomorrow I would bury him in his shirt'; and I did. And let me advise you to do so by Sir Christopher."

"*You* look delicate, now. Let me recommend you to take camomile tea in a morning, fasting. Beatrice is so strong and healthy she never takes any medicine; but if I had had twenty girls, and they had been delicate, I should have given them all camomile tea."[31]

Best of all is the famous Mrs Linnet.

'Mrs Linnet had become a reader of religious books since Mr Tryan's arrival, and as she was in the habit of confining her perusal to the purely secular portions, which bore a very

[31] 'Mr Gilfil', v.

small proportion to the whole, she could make very rapid progress through a number of volumes. On taking up the biography of a celebrated preacher, she immediately turned to the end to see what disease he died of; and if his legs swelled, as her own occasionally did, she felt a stronger interest in ascertaining any earlier facts in the career of the dropsical divine – whether he had ever fallen off a stage-coach, whether he had married more than one wife, and, in general, any adventures or repartees recorded of him previous to the epoch of his conversion. She then glanced over the letters and diary, and wherever there was a predominance of Zion, the River of Life, and notes of exclamation, she turned over to the next page: but any passage in which she saw such promising nouns as "small-pox", "pony" or "boots and shoes" at once arrested her.'[32]

Mrs Linnet's way of reading 'good books' would not be a bad way of rereading George Eliot. The novels must be read all through at least once, but when one knows how everything falls into place there is much that one will not care to read again.

The polysyllabic humour and the scientific language are exceedingly tiresome. 'Indeed what mortal is there of us, who would find his satisfaction enhanced by an opportunity of comparing the picture he presents to himself of his own doings, with the picture made on the mental retina of his neighbours? We are poor plants buoyed up by the air-vessels of our own conceit: alas for us, if we get a few pinches that empty us of that windy self-subsistence.'[33]

Leslie Stephen pays her a back-handed compliment when he says: 'George Eliot's background was always so scientific and philosophical that it would have been difficult to be quite free from the taint. The weakness does not imply affectation, and should be taken as an implied, if undeserved, compliment to the reader's intelligence.' The compliment, however, if undeserved is also undesired, and a 'taint' it remains. It may be attributed not only to her later environment, but also to her early life as an autodidact: she did not know how much the ordinary educated person might be expected to know, and therefore her references were without tact.

[32] *JR*, iii.
[33] 'Amos Barton', ii.

We owe a debt of gratitude to the first readers of the *Scenes* who so greatly over-rated them. But for their excessive praise George Eliot would have been discouraged, and we might have had no more fiction from her. They did not appear in a golden decade, but Dickens and Thackeray were still writing. Though Kingsley and Charles Reade were propagandist and boring, there were Trollope and Mrs Gaskell. A critic of George Eliot[34] says that he would hesitate to say that the *Scenes* were better than *Cranford* or *Barchester Towers*. Few people would hesitate to say that they were much inferior by Jane Austen's standard of 'work in which the most thorough knowledge of human nature, the happiest delineation of its varieties, the liveliest effusions of wit and humour are conveyed to the world in the best chosen language' – and too often the language could hardly be worse chosen.

---

[34] Thomas A. Noble, *Scenes of Clerical Life* (Yale, 1963), p. 18.

II   Adam Bede

'The little germ' of *Adam Bede* (as Henry James would call it) was an incident in the life of George Eliot's aunt Mrs Samuel Evans, a methodist preacher. Mrs Samuel Evans had once spent the night in prison with a girl convicted of child-murder, she had prevailed on the girl to make a confession of her guilt, and had next day accompanied her to the place of execution. George Henry Lewes said that the incident would make a good scene in a novel, and Adam Bede was designed round it. George Eliot's imagination was still moving in the Warwickshire of her youth, and she had been thinking of writing another Clerical Scene.

The prison scene naturally required two characters – Dinah Morris, the Methodist preacher, and Hetty Sorrel, the seduced village girl. A seducer also was indispensable, and Arthur Donnithorne, a young militia officer and heir to the village squire, was fitted to the role by popular tradition. Moreover it had to be someone brought into contact with Hetty by village life – for George Eliot rightly maintained unity of atmosphere – and yet someone who could not be expected to marry her. The date of the story is 1799–1807: too late for the young man to have had the cheerful irresponsibility of Tom Jones about the begetting of bastards, or for respectable country-folk like the Poysers to think lightly of Hetty's fall. But the date was most probably fixed by that of Mrs Evans's adventure, which took place in March 1802.

George Eliot thought that the prison scene would be more touching (moreover it thus arises more naturally from the story) if the two young women were antecedently connected: she therefore made Hetty the niece of a farmer, Martin Poyser, and Dinah the niece of his wife. Hetty was to be given an honourable lover in her own walk of life, also for greater pathos: he was Adam Bede, a carpenter who had many of the characteristics of the author's own father. George Eliot's interest in clerical life caused her to give an important and sympathetic role to the local clergyman, Irwine, vicar of Hayslope and Blythe and rector of Broxton. The other characters, to use the Jamesian definition, belong more to the 'treatment' than to the story. Though Dinah and Hetty are orphans, they have the Poyser household as a background, and Adam Bede, Arthur Donnithorne and the Rev. Adolphus Irwine are all equipped with relations; and other villagers of Hayslope have small parts.

The love-story, trivial in plot, is often disparaged, and it is at once evident that Lewes's advice was mistaken – but George Eliot had not yet tackled a long novel, and she did not quite know what was involved. Moreover she had Scott too much in mind, particularly *The Heart of Midlothian*. Nevertheless there are interesting features in the story as she treated it; and, as it is the central theme, we must take a poor view of the book if we treat it with contempt.

Arthur Donnithorne is not a callous rake, nor is he an oaf like Tom Jones. His first appearance is good: 'If you want to know more particularly how he looked, call to your remembrance some tawny-whiskered, brown-locked, clear complexioned young Englishman whom you have met with in a foreign town, and been proud of as a fellow-countryman – well-washed, high-bred, white-handed, yet looking as if he could deliver well from the left shoulder and floor his man' (ch. 5). Adam had been his hero as a boy, and Irwine had been his tutor; they both remained strongly attached to him. His intentions of being a better landlord than his grandfather when he succeeded to the property were not only good, but well-informed, and the tenants were looking forward to his replacing the stingy old squire. The Poysers were no exception.

For some time Arthur has been attracted by glimpses of Poyser's niece, Hetty, and she is successfully presented as being distractingly pretty. Physical beauty, impossible to render by direct description – in which it is merely boring – is here conveyed by analogy: hers was a beauty 'like that of kittens, or very small downy ducks making gentle rippling noises with their soft bills, or babies just beginning to toddle and to engage in conscious mischief' (ch. 7). Arthur, who has seen her in church and elsewhere and has shown some notice, is first heard speaking to her while she is making butter in her aunt's dairy, a very becoming occupation. He is soon going to celebrate his twenty-first birthday, and has every excuse to ask the niece of his grandfather's best tenant to promise him a dance on that occasion. He has less excuse to find out that she often walks through the grounds at Donnithorne Chase to visit his aunt Lydia's maid, Mrs Pomfret, who is teaching her lace-mending.

Arthur's obvious admiration had already induced in Hetty a languid and dangerous 'Bovarisme' and day-dreaming. His glances produced 'a pleasant narcotic effect' and he was always finding excuses for calling at the Hall Farm 'and always would contrive to say something for the sake of making her speak to him and look at him' (ch. 9). She had as yet no idea that she could be loved by him, but was already numbed as regards other feelings. She was lazy about her duties and impatient with her aunt's children – in any case she cared nothing for children or other young creatures (ch. 15). We see her cross and pettish – as those whose minds are not present, but are occupied with an absent object (and one that is no good to them) are very likely to be. 'If Hetty had been plain' (we are told on one such occasion) 'she would have looked very ugly and unamiable at that moment, and no one's moral judgment upon her would have been in the least beguiled' (ch. 23). She is an early and elementary example of the numb 'torpedo', who will appear more horribly as Rosamond Vincy.

Irwine warns Arthur against turning Hetty's head by his notice, but ironically, in the course of the same conversation (ch. 9) he expresses the hope that Adam, now freer on account of his father's death, will marry an excellent girl, Mary Burge. Had he been well enough informed to tell Arthur that Adam was in love with Hetty, she would have been quite safe from the generous young man.

Meetings between Arthur and Hetty took place in the Chase, and were at first innocent and almost idyllic. Arthur suddenly became aware of his desire when his arm first encircled Hetty and her basket fell on the ground 'with a rattling noise' (ch. 13). After their first kiss, Arthur felt really uncom-

fortable about the whole affair and decided to confide in
Irwine.

He had already made an attempt to get out of temptation's
way. He was a moral character. 'Nature has taken care that he
shall never go far astray with perfect comfort and satisfaction
to himself: he will never get beyond that borderland of sin,
where he will be perpetually harassed by assaults from the
other side of the boundary' (ch. 12). But one of the horses was
lame, and he could not go on the visit that he planned,
accompanied by his servant. If his grandfather had been less
mean about his stables, he would not have been kept at home
in this way.

When he rode over to breakfast with Irwine, he intended a
sort of unsacramental confession as a way of wrestling with
temptation. His advances towards admission, his vacillation
and retreats are movingly conveyed. George Eliot is for the
first time engaged with one of her favourite themes.

Arthur gets near to the point. "But surely you don't think a
man who struggles against a temptation into which he falls at
last as bad as the man who never struggles at all?" (ch. 16).

"No, my boy, I pity him in proportion to his struggles, for
they foreshadow the inward suffering which is the worst
form of Nemesis. Consequences are unpitying. Our deeds
carry their terrible consequences quite apart from any fluctua-
tions that went before – consequences that are hardly ever
confined to ourselves."

In this speech there is George Eliot's characteristic device of
prophecy, which she constantly uses (and sometimes abuses)
to emphasise her story; there is also a statement of that
approximation to Self-Determinism, the ineluctability of
consequences, that was central to her philosophy. The future
seduction of Hetty, her pregnancy and confinement are the
clearest possible illustrations to the text 'As a man sows, so
shall he reap'. Nevertheless, the element of Free Will is also
there. Irwine awaits the confession from Arthur to which this
discussion seems to have been leading. Arthur hangs back,
perhaps because of 'the fear lest he might hereafter find the
fact of having made a confession to the Rector a serious
annoyance, in case he should *not* be able quite to carry out his
good resolutions? I dare not assert that it was not so. The

human soul is a very complex thing.' Out of delicacy, Irwine
refrains from pressing him: a fatal omission.

The visit to Irwine did Arthur this much good that he
dragged himself away for a fishing holiday; but on his return
he continued to dally with Hetty, and he gave her a pair of
garnet and pearl ear-rings and a locket. This locket she wore
inside her frock at the celebration of Arthur's coming-of-age
on 30 July. Mrs Poyser's little girl broke the string, and it fell
to the ground and was seen by Adam.

George Eliot is always modest and restrained when writing
about sex – her publisher was puzzled for quite a long time
about Mrs Transome's past in *Felix Holt*. In *Adam Bede* we are
further kept in the dark. We do not know when Hetty's seduction took place, nor if there were repeated acts. Certainly it had
not taken place before 30 July, when Arthur had only 'gone a
little too far, perhaps, in flirtation' (ch. 24). We may think it
not improbable that it happened at the *rendez-vous* that he gave
her for two days later (ch. 26). It certainly occurred before
18 August, and no doubt in the hermitage, a little retreat of
Arthur's in the park, where Hetty left a pink silk handkerchief
behind. On 18 August Adam sees the two lovers kissing in the
Chase; he fights Arthur – although Arthur had no idea that
he was doing him any wrong. He insists on Arthur breaking
with Hetty and writing a letter to undeceive her, in case she
has any hopes of becoming his wife.

Arthur's was a 'loving nature'; he was sincerely grieved at
the wrong done to Adam (though it was done in ignorance, and
would not have been done except in ignorance) and at the
pain that he must inevitably give Hetty. 'He found out the
dream in which she was living – that she was to be a lady in
silks and satins', but he hoped later to make up to her for her
disappointment. Something of his 'freshness of feeling' had
gone. 'Our deeds determine us as much as we determine our
deeds. . . There is a terrible coercion in our deeds which may
turn an honest man into a deceiver, and then reconcile him to
the change. . . No man can escape this vitiating effect of an
offence against his own sentiment of right' (ch. 29).

Arthur was now faced with the one moral problem of the
book. He felt with sorrow that he was obliged by his past wrong
actions to deceive Adam into thinking the flirtation had not

gone far: 'It was the only right thing to do.' Probably, in the circumstances, it was; but he felt a sudden dread 'lest she should do something violent in her grief', and upon that dread came another, 'which deepened the shadow'. Arthur, it would appear, was considering the possibility of her pregnancy, which she, like a little natural animal, may never have imagined.

'To be sure, Adam was deceived – deceived in a way that Arthur would have resented as a deep wrong if it had been practised on himself.' But it was Arthur's duty to protect Hetty as far as he could, and the truth was not owed to Adam, who was not her affianced lover. Arthur did not go away without leaving Hetty an address, and he was quite reassured when he heard from Irwine in December that she was to be married to Adam in March (ch. 44). He had then a right to feel that any harm he had done was now undone. The terrible consequences of his sin were only known to him when he returned from Ireland – where he had gone with his regiment – to attend his grandfather's funeral.

Arthur's letter roused Hetty from her animal well-being and her wishful thinking. The violence of her emotion is comparable to that of a heroine infinitely superior to her in mind and character. Her terrible night and morning at the Hall Farm make one think of Marianne Dashwood in Berkeley Street, after the reception of Willoughby's infamous letter in Jane Austen's *Sense and Sensibility*. Having wept away all her tears, she rises in 'that dry-eyed morning misery, which is worse than the first shock, because it has the future in it as well as the present' (ch. 31).

Hetty is not large enough for tragedy, but she is very much more than pathetic. George Eliot, like Jane Austen, has gone almost as far in depicting pain as the reader will endure. But Hetty is a small person; her vanity has received a deeper wound than her heart. She begins to find comfort in the kindness of Adam, 'who knew half their secret' (ch. 29). She received the letter of farewell on 21 August, and was betrothed to Adam on 2 November.

The next three months was a busy time for Adam, and he saw little of Hetty; he was worried because she sometimes seemed unhappy. George Eliot has been so delicate about Hetty's pregnancy that (despite a few hints) someone who did not know the story might hardly suspect it on a first reading, until it burst on him as a shock (as on Adam and Arthur) when she was arrested on a charge of infanticide. If the author intended this, it was not a good idea. We follow Hetty with less understanding and sympathy – and she is not a person who commands sympathy in herself. No one would wish for outspokenness – as inappropriate as mystery in this book – but the mystery could have been abolished in a phrase or two which would not have prevented Queen Victoria from reading (as she did) *Adam Bede* to the Prince Consort.

In the second week in February Hetty left home on the pretext of a visit to Dinah, to persuade her to come to the wedding. In fact she intended to make her way to Windsor, where she believed Arthur still to be stationed. She had not thought of writing to him, and had not heard (though Adam knew) that the Loamshire militia had gone to Ireland. Her only hope was to be looked after and hidden 'and a hidden life, even with love, would have had no delights for her' (ch. 36), for it would offer nothing to her vanity – and we may be sure that love would not last long in the circumstances.

She had very little money, and she had the pride 'not only of a proud nature, but of a proud class – the class that pays the most poor-rates, and most shudders at the idea of profiting by a poor-rate'. She prolonged her journey by going to Stratford-on-Avon in error for Stony Stratford – behaving for once like a Hardy character.

At Windsor, where her landlady 'looked at her ringless hand', Hetty learned of Arthur's departure. She left his presents, the ear-rings and locket, as a pledge. In her 'journey in despair', in search of death and in fear of it, Hetty is almost completely depersonalised: she has become suffering itself, and weariness. She no longer looks much like the person we know, and we seldom hear her words. Even now, George Eliot still seems to have her knife into her: 'Poor wandering Hetty, with the rounded childish face, and the hard, unloving, despairing soul looking out of it – with the narrow heart and narrow thoughts, no room in them for any sorrows but her own, and tasting that sorrow with the more intense bitterness!' (ch. 37). It is hardly a moment for her to be thinking of other people's lesser troubles. But in spite of the author's lack of sympathy, the whole chapter is a triumph as a picture of inarticulate misery.

While Hetty is Martin Poyser's niece, Dinah is the niece of his wife. When the book opens she is at Hall Farm on a visit from the neighbouring county of Stonyshire – that harsh, industrial county is favourable to Methodism, while prosperous, agricultural Loamshire is unpropitious. We first see her preaching on the green at Hayslope, and through the eyes of a man on horseback (a Walter Scott figure unless, as is more probable, he derives from G. P. R. James), who hitherto knew 'but two kinds of Methodist – the ecstatic and the bilious' (ch. 2). He promises to be more important than he will turn out to be; he reappears as Colonel Townley, the governor of Stoniton jail – where he admits Dinah to Hetty's condemned cell. It would be easy to dispense with him.

Dinah appears at once as good, and not unlikeable. Her sermon is perfectly simple – though somewhat 'ecstatic' – and, unlike those of poor Amos Barton it is completely adapted to the intelligence of her audience – for she had, as he had not, that gift of sympathy, on which George Eliot set so much store. Again, unlike Amos Barton's 'ordinary tones', her 'mellow treble tones' had 'a variety of modulation like that of a fine instrument' – but of course, as we cannot hear them, she and Amos neither win nor lose our sympathy on account of their voices. It is a pity that when talking to her aunt, Rachel Poyser, to Lisbeth Bede, or to Mr Irwine she should be made to use so much 'Methody' jargon, when her preaching is so free from it; in consequence her conversation is boring and without charm. Nevertheless her worth is established. She is far more useful at Hall Farm than Hetty; she comforts Lisbeth Bede after her husband's death (in which Hetty takes no interest), and Mrs Poyser's little girl who 'takes against Hetty' (ch. 14) is happy to be held in Dinah's arms.

Dinah returns from her errand of mercy to Lisbeth Bede, just as Hetty returns from her first meeting with Arthur in the wood. That night Dinah feels a painful anxiety about Hetty and an urge (she calls it 'guidance') to go to her room.

"Dear Hetty," she says, "it has been borne in upon my mind tonight that you may some day be in trouble – trouble is appointed for us all here below, and there comes a time when we need more comfort and help than the things of this life can give. I want to tell you that if ever you are in trouble and need a friend that will always feel for you and love you, you have got that friend in Dinah Morris at Snowfield" (ch. 15).

Dinah's words were as prophetic as the speech uttered next day by Irwine to Arthur. They only frightened Hetty – though neither she nor Dinah can have taken the words 'in trouble' in the idiomatic sense, in which the reader is to understand them. These two prophecies, almost simultaneous, are another of those instances where the bone-structure of the book shows too clearly through the flesh.

A similar contrivance is shown a few weeks later, when on 21 August Dinah's pious letter to Seth Bede, who is unsuccessfully courting her, is handed by him to his brother Adam – who that same evening gave Hetty Arthur Donnithorne's letter of farewell.

The Poysers sent at once for Dinah on hearing of Hetty's arrest, and she at once went to Stoniton. It had been partly in search of her that Hetty had ended her wanderings near that town, where she had given birth to her child in the night of 27–8 February, and where she was now in jail. Dinah reached her on Friday night (13 March); her execution was set for the next Monday morning.

In the prison scene Dinah prays and preaches with eloquence, but it is Hetty who is moving. Holding on to Dinah's hand in the dark, she breaks through the frozen reserve that has shut her off from all human sympathy since her arrest – but we may doubt if it is the prayer and preaching that have won her, and not just the warm human presence. It is natural that Irwine should have seemed too remote from her to be able to do anything for her.

Hetty is not absolutely guilty of murder: she did not kill her child but abandoned it, half-buried in chips and turf. She went back because she was haunted by its crying, but it had been removed. "Dinah, do you think God will take away that crying, and the place in the wood, now I've told everything?" (ch. 45).

The scene is powerful, and yet its only place in a novel is at the end. George Eliot was being led astray by 'real life' – as

Stendhal was in *Le Rouge et le Noir*. Leslie Stephen rightly contrasted Dinah, and to her disadvantage, with Jeanie Deans in *The Heart of Midlothian* – a far more interesting character, who obtained her sister's pardon by a heroic walk to London. George Eliot's *donné*, the story of Mrs Samuel Evans, was much less fit for expansion into a novel than that of Scott – but it is not at all unlikely that she had Scott in mind when she yielded to Lewes' advice.

If Hetty were to be hanged (as her original had been) then her confession might give us a melancholy satisfaction. We should not quite convict her of murder, nor should we so far acquit her as to be revolted by injustice. We could feel that she had died in peace. But her execution would be an abominable and inartistic shock: George Eliot would be breaking faith with us if she allowed it to occur. An author who has created a butterfly must not break it upon a wheel. She has got herself into an impasse which requires the clumsy device of a *deus ex machinâ*. The part is played by Arthur riding up to the scaffold 'carrying in his hand the hard-won release from death' (ch. 47).

Adam Bede, the honourable lover, is successfully presented as an honest and intelligent craftsman; he is in part inspired by George Eliot's father, out of whom she was to make a more interesting character in Caleb Garth of *Middlemarch*. He was an afterthought to the original story, and it was a mistake to blow up his very minor part until he became the eponymous hero of the book. He is frequently sentimentalised: 'the big, out-spoken fearless man' who was 'very shy and diffident as to his love-making' (ch. 23); 'the strong man, accustomed to suppress the signs of sorrow' (ch. 38); 'this brave, active man' (ch. 42); 'the strong dark-eyed man' on whom Dinah was to turn her 'mild gray eyes in love!' (ch. 54).

Lewes had thought Adam too passive, and indeed it might have been better to have left him more like his brother Seth, and to suppress Seth, who would not be missed. Adam certainly begins by being dumbly enslaved by Hetty, and goes on as he has begun. It was perhaps Lewes's advice working on her that made George Eliot see of herself the fight between Arthur and Adam as a *necessity*: this thought came to her while she was listening to *Wilhelm Tell* at the Munich opera.

As was her way, she prepared for the fight by a 'prophecy', a trick of tragic irony that she may have learned of Greek drama.

We saw on his first appearance that Arthur looked 'as if he could deliver well from the left shoulder and floor his man'. But he says to Adam: "I could hit out better than most men at Oxford. And yet I believe you would knock me into next week if I were to have a fight with you" (ch. 16).

The encounter is far better prepared by a very fine 'objective correlative': 'Notwithstanding his desire to get on, he could not help pausing to look at a curious large beech which he had seen before him at a turning in the road, and convince himself that it was not two trees wedded together, but only one. Foɪ the rest of his life he remembered that moment when he was calmly examining the beech . . . The beech stood at the last turning before the Grove ended in an archway of boughs that let in the eastern light; and as Adam stepped away from the tree to continue his walk his eyes fell on two figures about twenty yards before him' (ch. 27). This fixes the scene on our memory, as did the rattle of Hetty's work-basket that fell to the ground when Arthur first embraced her.

For all that, the fight is no *necessity*, and is not justified by the exigencies of plot or character. Adam was not an accepted lover and had no other claim to set himself up as Hetty's protector. Arthur, who believed him to be courting Mary Burge, had done him no intentional wrong and had no obligation to answer him. He himself admits this after the fight: "I'd no right to speak as if you'd known you was doing me an injury: you'd no grounds for knowing it; I've always kept what I felt for her as secret as I could" (ch. 28).

It is unpleasant for Arthur to lie to Adam when he demands (and by no right) how far things had gone between him and Hetty. And for Arthur to feel qualms about such a deception, after having seduced her, makes one think of the young man invented by Oscar Wilde who became a liar because he had done murder. The author is so anxious to build up Adam as a man who has been intolerably wronged, that she has managed to pull the wool over many of her readers' eyes, and perhaps her own. It is not the case that Arthur is high-handedly bestowing his leavings on Adam, after exercising the *droit du seigneur*. He does, and can do nothing to promote their marriage, but legitimately looks forward to it as a solution. Hetty possibly wrongs Adam from the first by her silence – but we do not know if in Hayslope virginity was as indispensable in a bride as it would be in a Greek island village. To Adam, perhaps it is, for he challenges Arthur: "Tell me she can never be my wife" (ch. 28). She certainly wrongs him later, by continuing her engagement without revealing her pregnancy. But of this Arthur is kept in total ignorance. He could have done little to atone, but he would have done what he could, as we know from his subsequent conduct.

Adam's marriage with Dinah at the end of the book was another of Lewes' unfortunate suggestions. To most readers it lacks interest, and to many it is quite unconvincing – it is a down-grading of Dinah from her mission, and this is made worse by her previous refusal of Seth (ch. 3). We feel that she did not really know herself, and was only waiting for a more attractive offer. Henry James would have preferred that the marriage should have been left as a possibility for the reader to guess at. It tidies the end of the book, and is of convenience to the author as the union of Adam and Hetty would have been to Arthur. It might, however have been better if the book had been concluded in summary, for all life goes out of it after Hetty's reprieve. No one could have complained if Adam – after a respectable interval – had married someone suitable like Mary Burge – a marriage about which we could not be expected to have any feeling.

It might be taken for granted that Adam should get over his love for Hetty, which was largely infatuation. Too much has been made of it. 'I think,' wrote George Eliot, 'the deep love he had for that sweet, rounded, blossom-like, dark-eyed Hetty, of whose inward self he was really very ignorant, came out of the strength of his nature, and not out of any inconsistent weakness. Is it weakness, pray, to be wrought on by exquisite music – to feel its wondrous harmonies searching the subtlest windings of your soul. . .? If not, then neither is it weakness to be so wrought upon by the exquisite curves of a woman's cheek and arms. . . For the beauty of a lovely woman is like music: what can one say more?' (ch. 33). One can say that it is not: that George Eliot, whom Lord David Cecil rightly called a Philistine, was almost invariably stupid about music as about the other arts. Her attitude to painting has already been seen, and Charles Eliot Norton wrote of the Priory: 'All the works of art in the house bore witness to the want of delicate artistic feeling or a good culture on the part of the occupants.'[1] Her own ugly style (and this passage will serve for an example) must make us question her taste in literature. Hetty's musical equivalent would be a pretty, catchy, popular song. She is nothing to do with exquisite music, and it is not the soul to which she makes any appeal. But the author is here, perhaps, trying to overcome her irritation at Adam's love for Hetty – what Leslie Stephen called 'the kind of resentment with which the true woman contemplates a man unduly attracted by feminine beauty'. And in this case the 'true woman' was remarkably plain.

Adam's was not the heroic kind of love that would have made him consent to father another man's child, and Hetty was evidently well aware of this. It never seems to have occurred to him to follow her into transportation, as the Chevalier des Grieux followed Manon Lescaut.

'It will be a country story – full of the breath of cows and the scent of hay,' George Eliot had said. Yet though Dr Leavis commands assent when he says that her picture of rustic life 'disposes finally of the Shakespearean Hardy' – for it is of rustic dialogue that he is thinking – nevertheless (though not Shakespearean) Hardy was a poet, as George Eliot emphatically was not, and he could convey the breath of cows and the scent of hay far better than she could.

Mrs Poyser, Dinah's aunt, is the model farmer's wife, as Adam is the model carpenter; her 'houseplace' is exquisitely dustless, her back-kitchen all it should be, and her dairy perfection, although she has to struggle against enfeebled health, and old Squire Donnithorne's stinginess about repairs to Hall Farm. As a comic character she has been overrated: her proverbial wisdom is never so funny as the Dodson sisters' talk in *The Mill on the Floss*. In this book George Eliot is not yet a mistress of dialogue, for Lisbeth Bede also utters apophthegms.

[1] Haight *Letters*, v, p. 8.

One feels that Mrs Poyser has been made a mouthpiece for a collection of saws that the author had by her, and adapted to their contexts; but when this suggestion was made by a reviewer it was indignantly denied. 'There is not one thing put into Mrs Poyser's mouth that is not fresh from my own mint.'[2]

"It's the flesh and blood folks are made on as makes the difference. Some cheeses are made o' skimmed milk and some o' new milk, and it's no matter what you call 'em, you may tell which is which by the look and the smell."

"I allays said I'd never marry a man as had got no brains; for where's the use of a woman having brains of her own if she's tackled to a geck as everybody's laughing at? She might as well dress herself fine to sit back'ards on a donkey."

"We shall all on us be dead some time, I reckon – it 'ud be better if folks 'ud make much on us beforehand istid o' beginnin' when we're gone. It's but little good you'll do a watering last year's crop."

(Of the head-gardener at Donnithorne Chase) "For my part, I think he's welly like a cock as thinks the sun's rose a-purpose to hear him crow."

She has, says Irwine, a tongue "like a razor", and she lets the old Squire have the edge of it when he wishes her husband to make an exchange of farms. But for all her quickness of temper, she is far less severe than others in judging Hetty, for whom her kind-hearted husband felt no compassion. 'We are often startled by the severity of mild people on exceptional occasions; the reason is that mild people are most liable to be under the yoke of traditional impressions' (ch. 40).

The Rev. Adolphus Irwine – 'Dauphin' to his old mother, a nickname which serves to make her still more regal – is, like Dinah, part of the conscience of the book. He was Arthur's tutor, and was nearly made his confidant about his growing obsession with Hetty. Adam always looks up to him, and in spite of Methodist pressure he will hear no other preacher. Poverty and the obligation to support two maiden sisters forces him to be something of a pluralist and condemns him to celibacy, though he is a 'handsome, generous-blooded clergyman' (ch. 5). He is scholar enough to have Aeschylus beside

[2] Haight *Letters*, III p. 25.

him at his breakfast table (ch. 16) – and one wonders if any genuine scholar dips into Aeschylus at breakfast time; the trait is perhaps copied from Fielding's Parson Adams rather than from life. His goodness of heart is finely illustrated by his tenderness to his invalid sister.

'Anne's eyes were closed, and her brow contracted as from intense pain. Mr Irwine went to the bedside, and took up one of the delicate hands and kissed it; a slight pressure from the small fingers told him that it was worth while to have come upstairs for the sake of doing that. He lingered a moment, looking at her, and then turned away and left the room, treading very gently – he had taken off his boots and put on slippers before he came upstairs. Whoever remembers how many things he has declined to do for himself, rather than have the trouble of putting on or taking off his boots, will not think this last detail insignificant' (ch. 5).

In spite of his scholarship (or because of it, for his scholarship was classical) he was no theologian. 'He felt no serious alarm about the souls of his parishioners, and would have thought it a mere loss of time to talk in a doctrinal and awakening manner to old "Feyther Taft", or even to Cranage the blacksmith. If he had been in the habit of speaking theoretically, he would perhaps have said that the only healthy form religion could take in such minds was that of certain dim but strong emotions suffusing themselves as a hallowing influence over the family affections and neighbourly duties' (ch. 5). He is akin to Maynard Gilfil of the *Scenes of Clerical Life*.

Irwine can hardly be blamed for doing nothing with Hetty who had never 'appropriated a single Christian idea or Christian feeling' (ch. 37). However, he succeeds in breaking Adam's vindictiveness against Arthur. "You have no right to say that the guilt of her crime lies with him, and that he ought to bear the punishment. It is not for us men to apportion the shares of moral guilt and retribution. We find it impossible to avoid mistakes even in determining who has committed a single criminal act, and the problem how far a man is to be held responsible for the unforeseen consequences of his own deed is one that might well make us tremble to look into it. The evil consequences that may lie folded in a single act of selfish indulgence is a thought so awful that it ought surely to awaken

some feeling less presumptuous than a desire to punish"
(ch. 41).

Arthur was no doubt far more guilty than Hetty of the child's
existence, but in no way guilty of its death. He voluntarily
punishes himself in the same way that the law punishes Hetty,
that is by the 'transportation' of military life. Irwine helps him
in this resolution, which he may have prompted. He is to have
the chief authority over the estate during Arthur's absence.
The young squire is going abroad, though at the cost of
resigning all his most cherished hopes, so that the Poysers may
not feel that they have to leave Hall Farm, and so that Adam
may remain in charge of the woods. It is a generous, perhaps a
sentimental action. It is true that Adam would not (at present)
much care to work for him, but the Poysers will none the less
have the embarrassment of living among people who know
that Hetty has been condemned to death.

Adam is intolerably severe: "The time's past for that, sir. A
man should make sacrifices to keep clear of doing a wrong;
sacrifices won't undo it when it is done. When people's feelings
have got a deadly wound, they can't be cured with favours"
(ch. 48).

Arthur controlled his anger: 'He could bear a great deal
from Adam, to whom he had been the occasion of bearing so
much' – the word 'occasion' is the just word, but it is not so
placed as to have a sufficient impact on the reader's judgment –
again the illusion of Adam as an intolerably wronged man is
revived. But Arthur does reprove him for his hardness.

Adam is won over, and this is intended to be the moral
climax of the book.

"I'm hard – it's in my nature. I was too hard with my
father for doing wrong. I've been a bit hard to everybody but
her . . . and when I thought the folks at the Farm were too
hard with her, I said I'd never be hard to anybody myself
again." He owns his own sin, harshness to his father: "I've
no right to be hard towards them as have done wrong and
repent."

This is a strange moral to be drawn out of (or forced on to)
the story of Mrs Samuel Evans, and one cannot help thinking
that Hetty's suffering has gone for very little, if a softening of
Adam is all that is to come out of it. George Eliot is almost

apologetic about this, and tells us that 'Adam could never cease
to mourn over that mystery of human sorrow' (ch. 54).

The author says: 'I aspire to give no more than a faithful
account of men and things as they have mirrored themselves
in my mind. The mirror is doubtless defective: the outlines will
sometimes be disturbed, the reflection faint or confused, but I
feel as much bound to tell you as precisely what that reflection
is, as if I were in the witness-box narrating my experience on
oath' (ch. 17). But if a novelist's mind is a mirror, even like
Stendhal's more famous 'mirror in the highway', the frame itself
composes and excludes.

George Eliot protested (almost as Jane Austen had, and with
much less right) that she did not want to create impossibly
good or bad characters, and insisted on Truth in fiction.
Unfortunately she seemed to think that meant 'the whole
truth' and that she was 'bound' (by what decree?) to include
dullness. We have seen her appeal to Dutch painting. Of this,
however, she had some aesthetic admiration – apart from the
moral and utilitarian reflections it inspired in her – and insofar
as it was aesthetic it was beneficial to her own art. The scene of
Hetty making butter (ch. 17) is a charming Dutch interior;
Dinah preaching on the green or the festivities at Arthur's
coming-of-age are *genre* pictures. But the scene of Arthur riding
up with the pardon is the worst sort of Academy picture.

It is a mistake that the author should use 'I' impersonally,
to bring in a narrator to talk to Adam Bede in his old age –
whether that narrator be the 'George Eliot' or the Marian
Evans of the Clerical Scenes. One of them he must be, for he
relates *Adam Bede* to the earlier book by his criticism of Irwine
and the zealous but 'sourish-tempered' Mr Ryde who succeeded
him (ch. 5). And it was time that George Eliot rid herself of the
habit of button-holing the reader, so much practised in her
first book, and not yet abandoned. 'Let me take you into that
dining-room and show you the Rev. Adolphus Irwine . . . We
will enter very softly, and stand still in the open door-way,
without awaking the glossy brown setter. . .' (ch. 5).

The powerful scenes of Arthur's temptation and Hetty's
agony lift the novel above what (in spite of the earnestness of
Mrs Samuel Evans) was a novelettish theme – to which

Adam's spiritual growth has been artificially attached. The 'breath of cows and scent of hay' are less omnipresent than the author intended. What remain in the memory as fine fictional inventions are Mr Irwine's boots and Adam's approach to the meeting in the Chase (both singled out by Blackwood for praise), the fall of Hetty's work-basket and 'the crying and the place in the wood'.

III   The Mill on The Floss

'To my feeling,' wrote George Eliot, 'there is more thought and a profounder veracity in "The Mill", but "Adam" is more complete, and better balanced. My love of the childhood scenes made me linger over them; so that I could not develop as fully as I wished the concluding "Book" in which the tragedy occurs, and which I had looked forward to with much attention and premeditation from the beginning.'[1]

It will be seen that while *Adam Bede* is uninterestingly drawn out after the prison scene, *The Mill on the Floss* is rushed to its conclusion. *Adam Bede* was faultily developed from a scene that would not bear development, and Adam as a character was unsuccessfully grafted on to the story. In *The Mill on the Floss*, however, Lewes is not to blame, and the faults are largely referable to the author's self-identification with the heroine. She was not at all like anyone in *Adam Bede*.

The end of the book, so often adversely criticised, was part of the original conception, and the epigraph, 'In their death they were not divided', had long been chosen. The author meant not only to represent the development (or rather the oscillation) of a powerful mind and soul situated in stiflingly provincial conditions, but also to show the unhappy love and estrangement of a brother and sister – her most important early experience. The reconciliation in death is not only a way of ending the story, but a kind of wish-fulfilment – the only possible non-incestuous consummation of fraternal love. For we have the illusion that people who die simultaneously die together, though Pascal has said: '*Je mourrai seul.*'

If they are to die together, their death must almost inevitably be an accident, and an accident cannot be really tragic: it is a happening that cannot come out of the people but has to be

---

[1] Haight *Letters*, III, p. 374.

joined on to them. It is impossible to see how that difficulty could be evaded.

Some preparation is provided. 'Fear death by water' is, from the beginning, the burden of Mrs Tulliver. Maggie says to Philip: "The first thing I ever remember in my life is standing with Tom by the side of the Floss, while he held my hand: everything before that is dark to me" (v. i) – as everything will be dark to her after their last embrace in the boat. St Ogg's preserves the legend of a boatman, something like St Christopher – and a remembrance of this enters into Maggie's mind on the Dutch vessel that picks up her and Stephen when they have been 'borne along by the tide'. We are aware of the water as the source of Mr Tulliver's livelihood, as one of the subjects of his self-destructive litigation, as the loved background to home at Dorlcote Mill (which is in fact on the tributary Ripple, and not on the Floss) and as the scene of social joys and sorrows at Lucy Deane's house. There it plays a positive role as accomplice in 'the Great Temptation', carrying Stephen and Maggie away with it. The author has done all she could – it is not possible, artistically, to make two of the chief characters in a novel die together.

The long-drawn-out beginning finely develops the stern, upright, manly Tom. He is not unlike a youthful Adam Bede; and after all, as Isaac (who was in part the model on which Tom was formed) was the son of Robert Evans (the part-model for Adam), a family likeness is natural. In contrast is the temperamental, sentimental, intellectual Maggie. She adores Tom, but while he is away at school she forgets to feed his rabbits and lets them die. Very likely the young Marian served Isaac thus; we may almost hope so, for Isaac needs some excuse.

Unfortunately there is a great deal of dialogue in the child-hood scenes, and in spite of her fine ear for the speech of simple people George Eliot never had any idea how to make children speak. Tom and Maggie are not so young as the adenoidal horrors of the Clerical Scenes or as Mrs Poyser's odious little Totty, whom Hetty may well be forgiven for detesting – but they are like children in children's books written by people who know nothing about them. Tom, the conventional brash schoolboy, is quite bad enough, but nothing to his arch little sister; even the intelligent Philip Wakem as a boy is as 'soppy' as any good boy out of the same sort of book. It is probably the case that very young persons should not in fiction be allowed to talk together for very long unless their conversation is to some extent stylised, as it has been by Ivy Compton-Burnett – and in some of her later books the stylisation is overdone.

George Eliot's children should be seen and not heard – and they are very effective to look at. The reconciliation – after the affair of the rabbits – is real and touching. 'Maggie's sobs began to subside, and she put out her mouth for the cake and bit a piece: and then Tom bit a piece, just for company, and they ate together and rubbed each other's cheeks and brows and noses together, while they ate, with a humiliating resemblance to two friendly ponies' (I. v). We also see Tom and Maggie sharing a jam puff; Tom helping her to shear her hair; Maggie pushing the pink-and-white Lucy into the mud; Maggie offering herself to the gipsies as their queen; Tom cutting his foot with old Poulter's sword.

The great attraction of the first part of the book is its fun – one will not say 'charm', for it is puzzling to find this word used (and by good critics) about an author so totally devoid of charm as George Eliot. Nowhere else is she so frequently and magnificently funny as here.

Mrs Tulliver's family, the Dodsons, are the chief fount of humour. They are carefully poised, near the top of the lower middle class, with a respectability which is honourable as well as absurd. They have a tradition of thrift and good-house-keeping, together with a considerable contempt for those who are not 'kin', and an extreme sensibility to their neighbours' good opinion. Sister Deane, a 'thin-lipped' woman, who has married an up-and-coming man, is the least developed: she will die betimes, leaving her daughter Lucy to become almost a lady, and a possible bride for Stephen Guest.

Sister Glegg plays the dominant role, as representing family justice, and is disliked by the young Tom and Maggie; but after Maggie's unfortunate escapade she is the one person who stands up for her. "*I* won't throw ill words at her – there's them out o' th' family 'ull be ready enough to do that. But I'll give her good advice; an' she must be humble" (VII. iii). She has precipitated Mr Tulliver's downfall by threatening to call in the money she had lent him, because she felt affronted at the first great gathering of the clan to discuss Tom's schooling. Nevertheless, she would have been content to let things lie; but Tulliver, with fatal obstinancy, paid her off, although he could not afford to do so. She comes to sit in judgment at the second gathering, after the downfall. Tom boldly asks the aunts to advance their future legacies to him and Maggie, so that their mother's things may not be sold up, and Mr Glegg upholds his brave speech.

"Yes, Mr Glegg . . . It's pleasant work for you to be giving my money away, as you've pretended to leave at my own disposal . . . and I've saved it and added to it myself, and had more to put out almost every year, and it's to go and be sunk in other folk's furniture and encourage 'em in luxury and extravagance as they've no means of supporting; and I'm to alter my will, or have a codicil made, and leave two or three hundred less behind me when I die. . ." (iii. iii). For the Dodson family cared most for posthumous respectability; their funerals were conducted with peculiar propriety, and their wills were both a model of family justice and a revelation of even greater prosperity than was attributed to them. Indeed one of Mrs Glegg's chief inducements towards a charitable view of Maggie was the hope that she need not find a family disgrace deep enough to oblige her to cut her niece out of her will.

The funniest is the lachrymose Sister Pullet who, having married a gentleman farmer, 'had leisure and money to carry her crying and everything else to the highest pitch of respectability'.

Even the display of a new bonnet to her Sister Tulliver started melancholy thoughts.

"Ah," she said at last, "I may never wear it twice, sister, who knows?"

' "Don't talk o' that, sister," answered Mrs Tulliver. "I hope you'll have your health this summer."

' "Ah, but there may come a death in the family, as there did soon after I had my green satin bonnet. Cousin Abbot may go, and we can't think o' wearing crape less nor half a year for him."

' "That *would* be unlucky," said Mrs Tulliver, entering

thoroughly into the possibility of an inopportune decease. "There's never so much pleasure i' wearing a bonnet the second year, especially when the crowns are so chancey – never two summers alike."

' "Ah, it's the way i' this world," said Mrs Pullet, returning the bonnet to the wardrobe and locking it up. She maintained a silence characterised by head-shaking, until they had all issued from the solemn chamber and were in her own room again. Then, beginning to cry, she said, "Sister, if you should never see that bonnet again till I'm dead and gone, you'll remember I showed it you this day" ' (I. ix).

There is no more need to see Mrs Pullet as a Dickensian inspiration than to think Dickens' Mrs Nickleby inspired by Jane Austen. Mrs Pullet, though a 'flat' character enough, keeps her place in the book and, though the greatest of them, is very much one of the Dodson tribe. Poor Mrs Tulliver, the feeblest of them, is yet recognisably one of the family: "As for them best Holland sheets, I should repent buying 'em, only they'll do to lay us out in. An' if you was to die tomorrow, Mr Tulliver, they're mangled beautiful, an' all ready, an' smell of lavender as it 'ud be a pleasure to lay 'em out" (I. ii). The Dodsons and the upper-class Lady Assher are sisters under the skin.

As well as her macabre humour, George Eliot introduces the humours of salesmanship (later admirably developed in *Middlemarch*). Riley, the auctioneer, obligingly sells Stelling as as tutor for Tom, almost out of a pure love for his profession of recommending articles for sale. 'Mr Riley knew of no other schoolmaster whom he had any ground for recommending in preference: why, then, should he not recommend Stelling? His friend Tulliver had asked him for an opinion: it is always chilling in friendly intercourse, to say you have no opinion to give. And if you deliver an opinion at all, it is mere stupidity not to do it with an air of conviction and well-founded knowledge. You make it your own in uttering it, and naturally get fond of it. Thus, Mr Riley, knowing no harm of Stelling to begin with, had no sooner recommended him than he began to think with admiration of a man recommended on such high authority, and would soon have gathered so warm an interest in the subject, that if Mr Tulliver had in the end declined to send Tom to Stelling, Mr Riley would have thought his friend . . . a thoroughly pig-headed fellow' (i. iii).

Such a passage is an example, also, of George Eliot's 'commentaries' at their best – for some word is required other than the Jamesian 'summary' and 'scene'. When they run away with her, they swamp the fiction – so that one critic has advised us to read *Romola* as a collection of essays. But here character (if of a generalised kind) is well and amusingly conveyed – it is easy to understand Proust's admiration of George Eliot.

The other piece of salesmanship is done in 'scene': a dialogue between Aunt Glegg and Bob Jakin the packman.

' "I'll say no more, mum; it's nothing to you – a piece of muslin like that; you can afford to pay three times the money for a thing that isn't half so good. It's nets *you* talked on, well, I've got a piece as 'ull serve you to make fun on . . ."

' "Bring me that muslin," said Mrs Glegg: "it's a buff – I'm partial to buff."

' "Eh, but a *damaged* thing," said Bob, in a tone of deprecating disgust. "You'd do nothing with it, mum – you'd give it to the cook, I know you would – an' it 'ud be a pity – she'd look too much like a lady in it – it's unbecoming to servants.' "

' "Fetch it, and let me see you measure it," said Mrs Glegg authoritatively' (v. ii).

This sales talk, like that of Riley, had an intimate connection with Tom's fortunes. Riley sold Mr Tulliver an education that was entirely useless to Tom.

> When land is gone and money spent
> Then learning is most excellent.

But when Tulliver's downfall comes, Tom's only asset acquired at his tutor's is a clear handwriting: Euclid and the Eton Latin Grammar are no good to him.

Bob Jakin's sales talk induces the Gleggs to advance Tom some money with which to trade in haberdashery, and this is his first step towards earning the money with which he will pay off his father's debts.

It was Bob Jakin who, with a job lot of old books, presented Maggie with *The Imitation of Christ*; she was ready for it. Her father had failed, and she was living in a dull misery that is worse than the tragedy to which it is a sequel. 'There is something sustaining in the very agitation that accompanies the first shocks of trouble, just as an acute pain is often a stimulus, and produces an excitement which is transient strength. It is in the slow, changed life that follows . . . in the time when day follows day in dull unexpectant sameness, and trial is a dreary routine, it is then that despair threatens. . .' (IV. iv). Something like this is anticipated in Hetty's 'dry-eyed morning misery'. It is a thing impossible to represent in drama, and very difficult in fiction, though superbly done by Proust, and by Balzac in *Eugénie Grandet*; few have done it better than George Eliot, and it is no wonder that many people find her depressing – she is.

It was an old book, marked in ink by 'some hand now forever quiet'. 'It was written down by a hand that waited for the heart's prompting: it is the chronicle of a solitary, hidden anguish, struggle, trust and triumph – not written on velvet cushions to teach endurance to those who are treading with bleeding feet on the stones. And so it remains to all time a lasting record of human needs and human consolations: the voice of a brother who, ages ago, felt and suffered and renounced – in the cloister, perhaps, with serge gown and tonsured head, with much chanting and long fasts, and with a fashion of speech different from ours – but under the same far-off heavens, and with the same passionate desires, the same stirrings, the same weariness' (IV. iii).

Balzac wrote of the *Imitation*: 'It is impossible not to be gripped by the *Imitation* which is to dogma what action is to thought . . . This book is a sure friend. It speaks to all passions, all difficulties, even those of this world; it resolves all objections, it is more eloquent than all preachers, for its voice is your own, that rises in your heart and that you hear in the soul. In short it is the gospel translated, made appropriate to every age, imposed on every situation.'[2]

The *Imitation* is indeed a stoical treatise, teaching the suppression of self-love, as Seneca had taught it. But the motive is different. It is of Christ that Thomas à Kempis taught the

[2] *Madame de la Chanterie.*

imitation, and Balzac rightly saw it as 'the gospel translated'. To George Eliot, re-reading it while she was writing the novel, it meant something very different from what it could have meant to Maggie, who read it together with the Bible and *The Christian Year*. She seems to forget this when she speaks of those who require 'something that will present motives in an entire absence of high prizes', for Thomas à Kempis (and in a passage marked by the 'quiet hand') offers 'an everlasting crown', and there is no higher prize.

The chief motive, after all, for detachment from self and from things and from persons is thereby to attain to attachment to God – otherwise stoical apathy is apt to be merely that state of 'indifference' which, as T. S. Eliot says 'resembles the others' (i.e. attachment and detachment) 'as death resembles life'. A renunciation that is not made for the love of God or our fellows merits Thackeray's comment on the *Imitation* (which he entirely misunderstood): 'The scheme of that book carried out would make the world the most wretched, useless, doting place of sojourn – there would be no manhood, no love, no tender ties of mother and child, no use of intellect, no trade or science.'[3]

Maggie was reading the *Imitation* with such lines as these of Keble's running in her head:

> The daily round, the common task
> Will furnish all we need to ask,
> Room to deny ourselves, a road
> To lead us daily nearer God.

John Wesley had sung:

> From Jehovah I am,
> For His glory I came,
> And to Him I with singing return.

George Eliot, his godless spiritual descendant, with a nonconformist conscience working on without theology, might have responded:

[3] Gordon N. Ray (ed.) (1945), *Letters and Private Papers*, II, p. 616.

From Nothing I am,
For Duty I came,
And to Nothing I grimly return.

Her attitude is unsteady. She appears in part to be almost jocosely apologising for the immature Maggie's need for belief when she says: 'In writing the history of unfashionable families, one is apt to fall into a tone of emphasis which is very far from being the tone of good society, where principles and beliefs are not only of an extremely moderate kind, but are always presupposed, no subjects being eligible but such as can be touched with a light and graceful irony' (IV. iii). But we hear also most clearly the heavy and clumsy irony of Miss Evans, envious of 'good society', from which she was still excluded, and of which she still knew very little – betraying herself by the sneering and vulgar word 'unfashionable'. The unsteadiness is disguised by an often-quoted passage which looks better out of its context. 'But good society . . . is of very expensive production; requiring nothing less than a wide and arduous national life condensed in unfragrant deafening factories, cramping itself in mines, sweating at furnaces, grinding, hammering, weaving under more or less oppression of carbonic acid – or else spread out over sheepwalks, and scattered in lonely houses and huts on clayey or chalky corn-lands, where the rainy days look dreary.' The truth of such social criticism is dramatically shown in many of Dickens's novels – but it has no relevance to the world of St Ogg's, where we look deeply into no life very high or very low in the social scale. George Eliot is preaching, because she does not quite know how to tell us that Maggie, in her unhappiness, has need of 'Enthusiasm'.

It is a very strange statement that 'Enthusiasm' offers no prizes and lies 'outside personal desire': the 'emphatic belief' needed by the unfortunate is surely belief in another world in which they will be compensated for the misery of their life on earth. It is on this point that revivalist religions have generally laid emphasis – an emphasis less characteristic of the 'superior clergy who are to be met with in the best houses'. For an after-life implies death, and in the best houses *O Mors, quam amara est memoria tua*! 'If we look carefully,' says an excellent critic,[4] 'we see that George Eliot makes the religious conversion' (of Maggie) 'insistently human: the value is that of selflessness; there is a conversion of ethic not belief.' This is the case – yet some of the citations from Thomas à Kempis imply a Deity, and the *Imitation* is read with Keble, and we are told of Maggie's 'new faith'. I think the truth lies in a compromise: George Eliot imagined (or refrained from fully imagining) Maggie's conversion as an experience similar to that of her own Evangelical youth, but tried to make the expression of it in the novel something that should conflict as little as possible with her views at the time of writing. Anything that so conflicted she could dismiss as not 'essential'.

In any case Maggie's conversion raises her to the level of those from whom much is required: she is one of those who seek perfection. Her temptations, her fallings from the higher standard and her returns to it, make her the most interesting 'case' among George Eliot's characters, and her story a 'problem novel'.

Her nature is understood and criticised: 'She threw some exaggeration and wilfulness, some pride and impetuosity, even into her self-renunciation: her own life was still a drama for her, in which she demanded of herself that her part should be played with intensity. And so it came to pass that she often lost the spirit of humility by being excessive in the outward act. . .' (IV. iii).

Presently temptation comes: it is not a simple temptation like that of Arthur Donnithorne, that should be rejected out of hand. It seems to take the form of a 'conflict of duties' – the pull on either side is so strong that the reader will not find it easy to say where the true duty lay.

Maggie again meets her brother's former fellow-pupil, her friend Philip Wakem, and he is the son of her father's arch-enemy. Are they to go on meeting? It will be convenient to tabulate the argument of this, the first or lesser temptation:

MAGGIE: We must not, I cannot hurt my father.
PHILIP: The hatred that lies between our fathers is unreasonable, and not worthy of respect.

[4] *Critical Essays*, p. 45.

MAGGIE: I'm quite sure that whatever I might do, I should
wish in the end that I had gone without anything for myself,
rather than have made my father's life harder to him . . .
Our life is determined for us – and it makes the mind very
free when we give up wishing, and only think of bearing
what is laid upon us, and doing what it is given us to do.
PHILIP: It seems to me we can never give up longing and
wishing while we are thoroughly alive. There are certain
things we feel to be beautiful and good, and we *must* hunger
after them. (v. i)

This is an argument directed straight at a sensitive and
noble soul like Maggie's. Moreover Philip is deformed, and
lonely in a philistine world. She may do him good: that is
always an argument for seeing people whom we ought not to
see – people far more deleterious than Philip can be to Maggie.

MAGGIE: ('It was so much easier to renounce the interest before
it came'.) To meet Philip, even if good in itself, implied
secrecy, 'and that would act as a spiritual blight'.

No doubt there must be volumes of Casuistry about Secrecy,
though Aristotle has nothing to say about it. Clandestinity
could be said, almost, to protect Vice, inasmuch as Shame
protects Virtue – but the parallel cannot go far. We are even
encouraged to do good by stealth. We know (from Newman,
if from no one else) that we do not owe the truth to every
impertinent enquirer, and that it may be a duty to lie like a
trooper: George Eliot did not hesitate to lie in defence of her
anonymity.
    And yet we may think (and we have probably observed)
that Secrecy is apt to act on a relationship as 'a spiritual blight',
and it may be doubted if it can be practised by those who would
be perfect. The counsel of perfection is that of Bishop Ken's
morning hymn, so dear to Adam Bede:

        Let all thy converse be sincere,
        Thy conscience as the noonday clear . . .

Philip offers her a book.

> MAGGIE: No thank you . . . It would make me in love with
> this world again – it would make me long to see and know
> many things – it would make me long for a full life.
> PHILIP: But you will not always be shut in your present lot:
> why should you starve your mind in this way? It is a narrow
> asceticism . . . Poetry and art and knowledge are sacred and
> pure.
> MAGGIE: But not for me – not for me . . . Because I should
> want too much. I must wait . . . this life will not last long.

The sides are well-balanced. Those who use foolish words
like 'life-affirming' or 'life-denying' will come out wholeheartedly on Philip's side . . . Others, perhaps, will say that a
single meeting with a friend out of the past ought not to make
Maggie go back on her resolution – not knowing, as Maggie
herself did not yet know, that renunciation is not a momentary
act, but may go on for a lifetime. And Philip overstates his
case – Poetry and art and knowledge may be pure – as things
to be sought for their own sake – but they are not sacred.
Overindulgence in them, as in any other good thing, may be
excessive or untimely – though of all Lucy Ashton's counsels of
perfection the hardest is: *Stop thine ear against the singer*.
   At their second meeting, Maggie forsakes the counsels of
perfection in favour of the standards of ordinary human life.
   The author takes sides against Philip, speaking of 'Maggie's
true prompting against a concealment that would introduce
doubleness into her own mind, and might cause new misery to
those who had the primary natural claim on her' (v. iii).
'Do not think hardly of Philip,' she begins. We are not likely
to do so. He was (as Maggie was not) in love, and he had no
reason to consider any member of the Tulliver family but her.
   'Secrets are rarely betrayed or discovered according to any
programme our fear has sketched out' (v. v). Aunt Pullet's
road from Garum Firs to Dorlcote Mill lay by the Red Deeps,
where Philip and Maggie were accustomed to meet. One day
she innocently mentioned that she often saw him there. Tom
knew that it was a favourite walk of Maggie's, and he forced the
truth out of her. He gave her the alternative of never meeting

Philip again, or of suffering him to tell her father. He forced her to go with him to a last meeting with Philip, and there poured cruel insults on Philip's deformity.

Maggie's reply to Tom is significant: 'Sometimes when I have done wrong it has been because I have feelings that you would be better for if you had them.' Tom is hard and a Pharisee; narrow and unbending. She could not feel that she was wholly wrong, or he wholly right; but she was conscious of a 'certain dim background of relief', for 'a deliverance from concealment was welcome at any cost'. Moreover the worst had happened, and was no more to be feared.

Three weeks later came the great climax to her family history. Tom paid back his father's creditors. Mr Tulliver assaulted Wakem, Philip's father, and died as a result of the exertion. 'Maggie said: "Tom, forgive me – let us always love each other"; and they clung and wept together' (v. vii). It could hardly be expected that at this crisis she should be spirited or adult enough to tell Tom that she would see Philip Wakem if she wished, now that it could not hurt her father any more.

Maggie is believed to contain a great deal of her author in her, and it may be so. But Maggie certainly differed from George Eliot, not in being an ugly duckling, but in turning into a swan. We do not see her again until two years later; in the mean time she had been teaching in a school. Now she comes to St Ogg's as the guest of her cousin, Lucy Deane. Lucy's mother is dead, and Mrs Tulliver lives with her as a house-keeper. Maggie has become a beauty. Long ago, in one of those prophecies in which the author delights, Maggie had complained to Philip that heroines were always fair-haired. ' "Well," said Philip, "perhaps you will avenge the dark women in your own person, and carry away all the love from your cousin Lucy. She is sure to have some handsome young man at St Ogg's at her feet now: and you have only to shine on him – your fair little cousin will be quite quenched in your beams" ' (v. iv). Maggie is strangely affected by this and (with prophetic irony) she is angry at the idea of being "odious and base enough to be her rival".

At the Deanes' house she meets Stephen Guest, who is almost engaged to Lucy, and Philip Wakem joins their musical parties.

Tom, who has exacted a promise that Maggie shall not meet him again, gives his reluctant permission. "But I have no confidence in you, Maggie," he says (VI. iv). "You're always in extremes – you have no judgment and self-command." Again: "I never feel certain about anything with *you*. At one time you have pleasure in a sort of perverse self-denial, and at another you have not the resolution to resist a thing you know to be wrong."

Tom understands Maggie very well, and it is perhaps inattention to his words that causes Dr Leavis to say that the 'soulful side' of Maggie is offered by George Eliot 'with a remarkable absence of criticism'. Tom is hard and insensitive, and cannot see far into her interior life, but he is aware of her emotional instability and her immaturity – he is never by his lights deliberately unjust. Maggie, however, is only eighteen, emerging from the treadmill of her life into comfort and young ladyhood at St Ogg's, and endowed with a new and widely admired beauty; there is quite enough to turn her head – and we have been told nothing about her spiritual progress during the last two years.

Maggie now finds herself an object of attraction to Philip Wakem, to whom she had once promised love (though imperfectly knowing what it was) and to Stephen Guest, who has all but promised love to her cousin Lucy. Like Arthur Donnithorne in his temptation, she enlists the clergyman on the side of her resistance. Dr Kenn (who probably owed his name to Bishop Ken, the author of Adam's hymn) is marked as a High Churchman by his name, and by the candlesticks that he has put on the altar; but he is otherwise very like the clergy of the Clerical Scenes.

' "O, I *must go*," said Maggie earnestly, looking at Dr Kenn with an expression of reliance, as if she had told him her story in those three words. It was one of those moments of implicit revelation which will sometimes happen even between people who meet quite transiently. . .'

Dr Kenn responded: ' "I understand," he said; "you feel it right to go" ' (VI. ix).

Stephen, sexually more roused than any other of George Eliot's characters, is seized by a violent impulse, and showers kisses on her arm; she repels him. She tells Philip that she must part from him because the only alternative is estrangement from her brother. "Is that the only reason that would keep us apart?" asks Philip, who has good reasons for thinking otherwise. She says that it is, and she believes it. 'At that moment she felt as if the enchanted cup had been dashed to the ground.' The cup of *Comus* one would suppose. 'The reactionary excitement that gave her a proud self-mastery had not subsided, and she looked at the future with a sense of calm choice.'

Like Arthur Donnithorne she was sexually tempted, as she had never been before, and like him she ran away – usually the wisest way of dealing with such a temptation. She went to her father's sister, Aunt Moss, which was exactly where she ought to have gone, and she was a delightful companion to her little cousins. Stephen followed her there. His plea was cogent, for neither of them was irrevocably pledged elsewhere. "It is unnatural: we can only pretend to give ourselves to anyone else. There is wrong in that too – there may be misery in it for *them* as well as for us" (vi. xi).

Maggie answers: "O it is difficult – life is very difficult! It seems right to me sometimes that we should follow our strongest feeling; – but then, such feelings continually come across ties that all our former life has made for us – the ties that have made others dependent on us – and would cut them in two . . . Many things are difficult and dark to me; but I see one thing quite clearly – that I may not, cannot seek my own life by sacrificing others."

For Sir Leslie Stephen the fault in this part of the book was that Stephen was a 'mere hairdresser's block, a woman novelist's creation, and totally unworthy of the passion of such a soul as Maggie's.' Bulwer Lytton thought that a girl so noble as Maggie could not stoop to accept the attentions of a man half-affianced to her cousin. But George Eliot insisted: 'Maggie's position towards Stephen is too vital a part of my whole conception and purpose for me to be converted to the condemnation of it'.[5]

Dr Leavis, while thinking no more highly of Stephen, very reasonably says: 'Stephen himself is sufficiently "there" to give the drama convincing force.' He can be imagined to have a

[5] Haight *Letters*, III, p. 327.

powerful sexual attraction, and we may perhaps apply to Sir Leslie Stephen his own words about Hetty; perhaps he feels 'the kind of resentment with which the true man contemplates a woman unduly attracted by masculine beauty'. Dr Leavis further goes on to say: 'There is no hint that, if Fate had allowed them to come together innocently, she wouldn't have found him a pretty satisfactory soul-mate.' Stephen might indeed be no worse a husband for Maggie than Ladislaw was for Dorothea. But I think there *is* a slight hint, given by Philip: "I have felt the vibrations of chords in your nature that I have continually felt the want of in his" (vii. iii).

Dr Leavis, however, wishes slightly to downgrade Maggie towards Stephen's level. In her presentment he sees the author as unself-critically indulging both in self-identification and self-pity. It may be conceded to him, perhaps, that Tom's criticism is insufficient. It seems likely that George Eliot made him finally more unsympathetic than she had originally intended – even such a softening trait as his childish fancy for Lucy is not developed. Nevertheless his 'Rhadamantine' sense of justice is not to be despised. Maggie's inner life is never looked at from outside. Dr Kenn, the only character capable of doing this, is not brought close enough. It is a clear case for one of the author's commentaries, but this is not forthcoming.

Maggie's cry to her Aunt Moss, after sending Stephen away, is an unconscious self-criticism. "I wish I could have died when I was fifteen. It seemed so easy to give things up then – it is so hard now" (vi. ix). When she was fifteen she did not know what 'giving up' meant.

Maggie went back to St Ogg's to stay with Aunt Glegg for protection from herself. But Lucy insisted on her coming over for evening visits, and Stephen could not keep away. Lucy believed her to be firmly attached to Philip, but he was made wretched by observing the 'mutual consciousness' between her and Stephen. A plan good-naturedly made by Lucy to allow Philip and Maggie a boating-excursion by themselves goes all wrong: it results in Stephen and Maggie being left alone together.

They are guiltless of the coincidence, but they take the boat, in the spirit of those who are to enjoy 'a last ride together' – a risk they know they ought not to take. Stephen, without noticing, passes Luckreth, the village where they always left the boat: he decides to go on. Maggie suddenly notices that she is in unknown country, and cries out. Stephen appeals to her to go on: everything has come about without their seeking. "We never thought of being alone together again: it has all been done by others. See how the tide is carrying us out – away from all those unnatural bonds that we have been trying to make faster round us – and trying in vain" (VI. ix). They will be carried to Torby, they can get a carriage to York, and thence to Scotland, where they can marry at once without waiting for a licence.

Maggie's reproaches are bitter; she feels that she has been trapped. Then she gradually yields to the pleasure of being 'borne along by the tide'. At length they hail a Dutch vessel, which will carry them northwards. Stephen is near her, and triumphant: 'There was, there *must* be, then, a life for mortals here below which was not hard and chill – in which affection would no longer be self-sacrifice.'

Maggie woke next day in misery: 'The irrevocable wrong that must blot her life had been committed: she had brought sorrow into the lives of others – into the lives that were knit up with hers by trust and love' (VI. xix). She thought of her earliest youth: 'She had renounced all delights then, before she knew them, before they had come within her reach. Philip had been right when he told her she knew nothing of renunciation: she had thought it a quiet ecstasy; she saw it face to face now – that sad patient loving strength which holds the clue of life – and saw that the thorns were for ever pressing on its brow.

'Too late! it was too late already not to have caused misery: too late for everything, perhaps, but to rush away from the last act of baseness – the tasting of joys that were wrung from crushed hearts.'

Stephen pleads: "The whole thing is done."

"No, it is not done," says Maggie. "Too much is done – more than we can ever remove the trace of. But I will go no further. Don't try to prevail with me again. I couldn't choose yesterday.

"There are memories, and affections and longings after perfect goodness, that have such a strong hold on me; they would never quit me for long; they would come back and be a pain to me – repentance. I couldn't live in peace if I put the shadow of a wilful sin between myself and God. I have caused sorrow already – I know – I feel it; but I have never deliberately consented to it."

(This is surely one of her definitely religious utterances.)

"I can't believe in a good for you, that I feel – that we both feel is a wrong towards others . . ."

Stephen says: "Admitting the very worst view of what has been done, it is a fact we must act on now; our position is altered; the right course is no longer what it was before."

The worst view will, of course, be taken by everyone at St Ogg's – with the exception of Dr Kenn, Mrs Tulliver, Mrs Glegg and the two sufferers, Lucy and Philip. Everyone else will believe that there was a deliberate elopement, and that Maggie and Stephen are lovers. Maggie herself knows 'that the consequences of such a fall had come before the outward act was completed'.

It is perhaps a pity that the 'outward act' was not completed. In consummated love with Stephen, Maggie might have found an ecstasy that 'doth unperplex'. She would have found it impossible to leave him, and there would be good reasons for not doing so. Maggie would have felt Stephen and herself spoiled for Lucy and Philip, and it would have been almost a duty to her family and herself to become 'an honest woman', as Stephen's wife.

She leaves Stephen, and it is the cruel amputating separation of two people who are physically very much in love. As in the Lesser Temptation, so now in the Great we may still ask if she is doing right. Can atonement now be made to Lucy and Philip by carrying out the old promises (which had not actually been made)?

Living in a later age, we cannot help being influenced by its permissiveness, even if we do not approve of it. Used as we are to hear of the break-up of marriages, we cannot help thinking nineteenth-century novelists took engagements a great deal too seriously – we cannot help wondering if Trollope is not making too much fuss over Lily Dale's 'disappointment', or if Henry James is not exaggerating the importance of that lamentable engagement in *The Spoils of Poynton*. In *The Mill on the Floss* it seems better that two people should be happy rather than that four should be miserable. It is true that Stephen did ultimately go back to Lucy, but that was years after Maggie's death. It is just conceivable that Maggie and Philip might have come together again, but only after 'a long while' (VII. iii).

The excellent clergyman Dr Kenn was obliged to entertain 'the idea of an ultimate marriage between Stephen and Maggie as the least evil' (VII. ii), and his is the most mature and enlightened conscience in the book. Certainly only such a marriage could render Maggie's position at St Ogg's tolerable, and the author will not say that he is wrong to accept such a possibility – only that he was right not to give advice.

'The question whether the moment has come in which a man has fallen below the possibility of a renunciation that will carry any efficacy, and must accept the sway of a passion against which he had struggled as a trespass is one for which we have no master-key that will fit all cases.' We must pass from the counsels of perfection of Thomas à Kempis to the case-law of the casuists.

Maggie might well feel that she could not trust Stephen. She does feel that any happiness she may enjoy with him will seem to have been stolen, and can therefore never satisfy her. Nevertheless the wrong to Philip and Lucy (such as it is) has been done, and will not be greatly aggravated if Stephen and Maggie profit by it. The reader would no doubt have felt that something of Maggie's higher nature was lost – that she was descending from the level of those who seek perfection, to the level of everyday life. The whole question is: what is the value of Maggie's aspirations to a higher life?

We cannot answer this question because, as the author said, the end comes too quickly. 'In fact the third volume has the material of a novel compressed into it.'[6] In any case, Maggie would have been too big for the book. With her oscillations she has the uncertainty of a character in life: while Adam Bede and Silas Marner move steadily towards greater charity for their fellow-men, Dorothea and Lydgate slump into mediocrity, and Gwendolen Harleth – an unpleasant young woman – is in training to be a saint after the end of the book. Maggie is so interesting a character that we can understand that the plot

[6] Haight *Letters*, III, p. 285.

has been sacrificed to her, and that, in consequence, the novel is a maimed masterpiece.

Back in St Ogg's, Maggie has to learn the true nature of renunciation. Stephen writes to beg her to recall him; her temptation has only begun. She has no previous experience of the misery of separation.

> *Que le jour recommence et que le jour finisse*
> *Sans que jamais Titus puisse voir Bérénice,*
> *Sans que de tout le jour je puisse voir Titus?*[7]

She is shaken by Stephen's letter. 'The leap of natural longing from under the pressure of pain is so strong, that all less immediate motives are likely to be forgotten – till the pain has been escaped from' (VII. v). Close within her reach lies happiness, and she is tormented by the feeling of Stephen's pain – which it is fully within her power to cure. Once she starts from her seat, after receiving his heart-broken letter, 'to reach the pen and paper, and write "Come!" ' She has already been forgiven by Lucy and Philip and feels sure that it is her duty to resist. She has now a time of pure mental suffering 'without active force enough even for the mental act of prayer'. Repeating the words of Thomas à Kempis, she accepts her cross.

"I will bear it, and bear it till death . . . But how long will it be before death comes! I am so young, so healthy. How shall I have patience and strength? Am I to struggle and fall and repent again? – has life other trials as hard for me still?"

Maggie then fell on her knees, and uttered her one prayer recorded in this book: "O God, if my life is to be long, let me live to bless and comfort" – and then the water rose.

Mrs Hardy[8] has well argued that in this novel there is always some relation to the author's problems. Maggie renounces a man who is bound by no social or legal ties: Stephen is not even officially engaged to Lucy, but he is not morally and emotionally free and Maggie cannot accept life with him except at the cost of pain to Philip and Lucy. George Eliot, on the other hand, accepted life with George Henry Lewes, who was legally

---

[7] Racine, *Bérénice*, IV, v.   [8] *Critical Essays*, pp. 50–1.

bound to an unfaithful wife, the mother of another man's children. She was not taking anything that belonged emotionally to any other human being; indeed she helped Lewes to maintain Agnes and her brood. Moreover she defied convention and became a social outcast because of her choice, while Maggie remained an outcast because of her refusal of the only way by which she could have gained acceptance at St Ogg's – that is, by becoming Stephen's wife.

Still more important is the story of brother and sister. Stephen has written a letter vindicating Maggie, Lucy has forgiven her, Philip trusts her, Mrs Tulliver has said: "You've got a mother." Bob Jakin and his wife have behaved admirably, as we should expect. Aunt Glegg's charity surprises us perhaps less than the author intended. Only Tom remains hard and unforgiving.

Isaac Evans held no communication with his sister till Cross had made her 'an honest woman', and (though she sometime professed indifference) there can be little doubt that she was profoundly hurt. It may have been the affections and pity that involved George Eliot in her various love affairs as much as sex, about which she is always diffident and shy. It is true that Meredith said 'the face with its long nose, the protruding teeth as of the Apocalyptic horse, betrayed animality' – he might have read it wrongly. Perhaps her strongest feeling was for Isaac.

The reconciliation in death may in part spring from the childish fantasy of saving the beloved, at great risk, from horrible danger. Maggie takes a boat and tries to save Tom from the flood: "Magsie!" he cries, in their old childhood language, and they die, clasped in a last embrace. George Eliot loved Maggie too much for any other ending – either a second-rate yielding, or a life of renunciation and shame; perhaps there was no possible artistic ending for this book.

IV Silas Marner

'It is a story of old-fashioned village life, which has unfolded itself from the merest millet-seed of thought.'[1] The 'little germ' of the book was a recollection of 'having once in early childhood seen a weaver with a bag on his back'.[2] George Eliot told Blackwood that he was 'a man with a stoop and expression of face that led her to think that he was an alien from his fellows'.[3]

It seems that she decided on the social regeneration of her stooping figure, and love was the natural force to employ for his recovery. Fortunately she did not this time choose the love of God as that force: indeed, at the outset Silas appears to be rejected by God and man. He was not a suitable subject for sexual love, nor was George Eliot at home in it as a writer. The introduction of a child was therefore almost inevitable, and a happy inspiration: as Wordsworth wrote in the lines from *Michael* that she chose for epigraph:

> A child, more than all other gifts
> That earth can offer to declining man,
> Brings hope with it, and forward-looking thoughts.

The two initial problems must have been to find out why Silas had become an alien, and then to introduce a child into his life.

The first was not difficult, and might be solved in many ways. George Eliot chose betrayal, one of the most isolating of experiences, as the cause of Silas's loneliness. His own familiar friend, William Dane, alienates the affections of his betrothed, and further causes him to be suspected of a theft which he himself committed while Silas was in a cataleptic fit. It may have been part of the original *donné* that the weaver should have fits – but, whether his catalepsy were due to life or to

---

[1] Haight *Letters*, III, p. 371.   [2] ibid., p. 282.   [3] ibid., p. 427.

invention, we cannot but think the author would have done better without it.

Silas and William are both members of a small dissenting congregation 'known to itself as the church assembling in Lantern Yard'. This congregation tries the case in its usual way by prayer and drawing lots. Silas submits to the test, in perfect faith that he will be cleared. The lots declare him guilty, and he goes out with his faith in God and man shattered.

'To people accustomed to reason about the forms in which their religious feeling has incorporated itself, it is difficult to enter into that simple, untaught state of mind in which the form and feeling have never been severed by an act of reflection. We are apt to think it inevitable that a man in Marner's position should have begun to question the validity of an appeal to the divine judgment by drawing lots; but to him this would have been an effort of independent thought such as he had never known; and he must have made the effort at a moment when all his energies were turned into the anguish of a disappointed faith.'

Silas went south, and set up his loom in a cottage near a deserted quarry. He came as a stranger, as a man of different physical type from the country-folk, practising the alien craft of weaving. Moreover his cataleptic fits and his knowledge of herbs rendered him uncanny in the eyes of the villagers of Raveloe. There was nothing to break in on his extreme loneliness.

The world of Raveloe, where the wars protected bad farming and men lived 'in careless abundance' (I. ii) was as far as 'good society' from that rude and arduous life based on 'the emphasis of want'[4] which has a crying need for 'enthusiasm' – it is the difference between Stonyshire and Loamshire over again. Silas now finds himself among people who needed 'nothing of that trust, which for him had been turned to bitterness'.

At first he began to work mechanically, and, needing something to love, he found it in the gold that he earned by his work. Thus fifteen years passed. During those years he had hardly any human contacts, and we do not hear him speak.

The story is organised like a fairy tale, with parallel themes.

[4] *MF*, IV, iii.

One of the squire's three sons robs Silas of his gold, another disowns his golden-haired child, and leaves her in Silas's arms.

George Eliot needed a child of about two years old, one who was just big enough to walk and to be looked after by the weaver, but yet too young to have any earlier memories. She would not have wished to repeat Hetty's story: the child's parents had been married, and she was not abandoned.

'A moment of compunction' had urged Godfrey Cass into a degrading marriage with a drunken barmaid, who was an opium addict. This had apparently taken place about eighteen months before her death, 'last Whitsuntide twelvemonth', when their child must have been six months old. 'It was an ugly story of low passion, delusion, and waking from delusion which needs not to be dragged from the privacy of Geoffrey's bitter memory' (I. iii). It is better that it should not be, for the delusion was partly due to 'a trap laid for him' by his brother Dunstan. If this story were to be convincingly developed it would take too long.

Godfrey had a gentle nature, and was in love with an excellent young woman. Furthermore he desired the order and decent domesticity typified by Nancy Lammeter and her family, as a contrast to the disorderly womanless Cass household. However he had weakly and viciously 'made ties for himself which robbed him of all wholesome motive and were a constant exasperation'. Worse, he had put himself into a position where he could be blackmailed by his brother – for a word to his father about the secret marriage would disinherit him. Dunstan pushes him to the extreme verge, for his wife also threatens exposure, and he may do as well to tell the squire himself. But 'the results of confession were not contingent, they were certain; whereas betrayal was not certain. From the near vision of that certainty he fell back on suspense and vacillation with a sense of repose.' He is the character without will-power or decision that George Eliot knows so well. Like Mr Micawber (whom he otherwise so little resembles) he waits for something to turn up; after all Dunstan has hinted that Molly might easily take a drop too much laudanum one day, and make him a widower.

We are in a world even humbler and more obscure than that of the earlier novels. The Lammeters are only well-to-do farmers. The greatest man in Raveloe is Godfrey's father, an uneducated small squire; nor has Godfrey any education. 'The subtle and varied pains springing from the higher sensibility that accompanies higher culture, are perhaps less pitiable than the dreary absence of impersonal enjoyment and consolation which leaves other minds to the perpetual companionship of their own griefs and discontents' (I. iii). Such was Godfrey's case.

Godfrey yields once more to threats on a day in late November, and allows Dunstan to sell his horse, Wildfire. Dunstan imprudently hunts the animal first, stakes it, and has to walk home. On the way back he thinks of borrowing money from the weaver, who is reported to have plenty hidden away, and may be bullied or cajoled into lending it to the squire's son.

By a series of coincidences the cottage is empty and un-attended: but they are sufficiently probable coincidences to give the story the solidity and authenticity it has, for all its air of being a fairy-tale. Silas had been given a small piece of pork and was roasting it over his fire on a string knotted round his door-key. He remembered that he had need of a very fine piece of twine and slipped out to get it without locking his door – for that would have entailed unknotting his key. His mind was at ease, for in all those years no one had attempted to rob him.

Dunstan wondered where the weaver was, and suddenly thought that he might have slipped into the quarry, which he had that morning observed to be full of red, muddy water. 'If the weaver was dead, who had a right to his money? Who would know where his money was hidden? *Who would know that anybody had come to take it away?*' (I. iv).

Throughout the book George Eliot is interested in the working of the people's minds; even from the first pages the reader notes the large number of words that express some form of intellection. As in *Adam Bede*, where Methodism is described as a 'rudimentary culture',[5] the author is concerned with such thought as is to be found in the comparatively unthinking. Godfrey's mental condition is analysed, and the same thing is done for Dunstan.

[5] *AB*, 3.

'A dull mind, once arriving at an inference that flatters a desire, is rarely able to retain the impression that the notion from which the inference started is purely problematic.' A true observation, though very ill expressed.

Dunstan searched for the hiding-place, which was betrayed by fingermarks on the sand that covered the brick floor. He found two leathern bags and seized them. He quickly closed the door behind him to shut in the light. 'The rain and darkness had got thicker, and he was glad of it . . . So he stepped forward into the darkness.' It was not until fifteen years later that his bones were discovered in the quarry, together with Silas's gold. No one had connected his disappearance – a thing which had occurred before – with Silas's loss. Only the reader knows the connection, and even he does not know what has become of Dunstan.

Silas runs with the news of his loss to the Rainbow Inn. The parlour is empty for its usual spirit-drinking customers have gone to a dance; the world of the kitchen, however, is occupied with its beer. The talk is convincing – a most remarkable achievement for a woman writer. The landlord proves himself fit for his office by a masterly power of agreeing with both sides in any argument; to stop disputes that are getting hot, he draws out the narrative gifts of old Mr Macey, the tailor and parish clerk. This is an ingenious contrivance of the author's for prompting the characters to say what she wants, but with an air of nature; old Macey required 'that complimentary process to bring him up to the point of narration' (I. vi) and 'he always gave his narrative in instalments, expecting to be questioned according to precedent'. The butcher also took part in the prompting.

Thus we easily arrive, through the reminiscences of an old inhabitant, at a ghost story, and thence at an argument about apparitions. The entrance of Silas in the middle of this talk seems like a proof of their existence.

Silas's loss brings him into better repute in Raveloe. This is in part due to sympathy with his misfortune (as Amos Barton's misfortunes endeared him to the people of Shepperton), and in part due to the removal of a superstitious prejudice against him. Silas cannot – as was thought – be in league with the Devil, for the Devil looks after his own. The wheelwright's wife, Dolly Winthrop, brings him a gift of cakes; she is the woman the village always calls in in cases of sickness. She preaches to him the simple theology of Raveloe, and tries to get him to church. The background is being set for the next change in his life.

Meanwhile Godfrey Cass's anxiety had reached a climax. He had been obliged to tell his father that he had handed some rents over to Dunstan, and he expected to be denounced for his secret marriage on his brother's return. He also expected his wife, Molly, to appear at any moment with her demands; and the squire was embarrassingly eager to promote his marriage with Nancy Lammeter. He recklessly enjoys the New Year ball at his father's house, as perhaps his last moments of pleasure.

Meanwhile Molly, in a spirit of revenge, was making her way there through the snow; she knew that 'the cause of her dingy rags was not her husband's neglect, but the demon Opium to whom she was enslaved, body and soul' (I. xii), but she chose to hide this from herself under bitterness towards Godfrey: '*He* was well off; and if she had her rights she would be well off too.' She collapsed and died in the snow, and the child woke and toddled to the open door of Silas Marner's cottage and soon was squatting in front of the fire, gurgling 'like a newly-hatched gosling beginning to find itself comfortable'. The newly hatched gosling is the most affectionate of little birds, ready to feel filial devotion to the first living creature it sees on emerging from the egg. It is therefore (as George Eliot must have known) exactly the right image for Eppie.

Silas had been going back and forth to the door in a listless way, almost wondering if his lost gold would return; at the door he had one of his cataleptic fits and lost consciousness. When he returned he found a heap of gold in front of the fire – the golden curls of the child. For a moment he thought it was the little sister he had lost in childhood. Later, after feeding her with porridge he saw that she wanted her wet boots taken off: she had come by natural means through the snow. He went out, and found her mother's body.

With the child in his arms he entered the Red House, while Bob Cass, the squire's favourite son, was dancing a horn-pipe.

He asked for a doctor, and said there was a woman, probably dead, in the snow. Godfrey recognised his child: 'There was one terror in his mind at the moment: it was that the woman might *not* be dead. That was an evil terror – an ugly inmate to have found a resting-place in Godfrey's kindly disposition' (I. xiii). The author apologises for him unnecessarily: only a saint could have wished to find his drugged and drunken blackmailer alive, and a saint would not have become involved with her.

In painful anxiety Godfrey followed his uncle, the doctor and Silas, and on the way they fetched Dolly Winthrop. The woman was dead, and Godfrey took a last look at his 'unhappy hated wife'. Silas, to everyone's astonishment, and even to his own, declared his intention of keeping the child.

Godfrey accounted plausibly enough for his presence on the scene, and the author's comment is very surprising. 'The prevarication and white lies that a mind that keeps itself ambitiously pure is as uneasy under as a great artist under the false touches that no eye detects but his own are worn lightly as mere trimmings when once our actions have become a lie.' It looks as if George Eliot is trying to elevate Godfrey on to the higher moral standard, and for no reason at all to provide him with a moral conflict – perhaps because there is no other in the book.

Godfrey can hardly at any time have kept his mind 'ambitiously pure'. His harmless 'white lies' are told to protect him from a curiosity that he had no obligation to satisfy. Arthur Donnithorne had been forced into a lie that was at least the suppression of a truth important to Adam. Godfrey's trivial 'prevarications' are no more than any of us might indulge in without uneasiness of mind to decline an invitation or to get rid of a bore. They are far less deceptive than the lies George Eliot constantly told to protect her anonymity. The 'ambitiously pure mind' of Newman would have been un-affected by them.

The child shows no sign of recognising him, and half-jealously Godfrey sees all its affection turn to Silas Marner. Godfrey 'would never forsake it; he would do everything but own it. Perhaps it would be just as happy in life without being owned by its father.'

Dolly Winthrop helps Silas to look after the child – she is a 'notable' woman and, though less aphoristic, has some likeness to Mrs Poyser. She stands godmother when the child is baptized (in case this has not been done before); it is named Hepzibah, after Silas's little sister, and is henceforth known as Eppie.

'. . . As the weeks grew to months, the child created fresh and fresh links between his life and the lives from which he had hitherto shrunk continually into a narrower isolation. Unlike the gold which needed nothing and must be worshipped in close-locked solitude . . . Eppie was a creature of endless claims and ever-growing desires, seeking and loving sunshine, and living sounds, and living movements; making trial of every-thing, with trust in new joy, and stirring the human kindness in all eyes that looked on her. The gold had kept his thoughts in an ever-repeated circle, leading to nothing beyond itself; but Eppie was an object compacted of changes and hopes that forced his thoughts forward, and carried them far away from their old eager pacing towards the same blank limit. . .' (I. xiv). Eppie is solid and actual, no dream child. George Eliot avoided motherhood for herself, and indeed she would have found it very inconvenient. No child of hers could have had Lewes as legal father, though he occupied that position towards the children that his wife Agnes bore to Thornton Hunt. But the Lewes boys called George Eliot 'Mutter', and she seems to have had no unsatisfied longings. Eppie was created out of her brain, not out of her need. Her gurgling monosyllables will no doubt charm the reader less than the author may have hoped – but she is once genuinely funny. Silas, with agony in his heart, has put her into the coal-hole as a terrible punishment. No sooner is she washed and dressed than she pops in again, peep-ing out to say: "Eppie in de toal-hole."

'There was no repulsion around him now, for young or old; for the little child had come to link him once more with the whole world. There was love between him and the child that blent them into one, and there was love between the child and the world . . .' Silas's reintegration is complete, and the chief part of the moral fable has been worked out.

George Eliot would not have believed that anyone but Wordsworth could have been interested in it, had not Lewes been 'strongly arrested'[6] by *Silas Marner*. It could indeed have been the subject for a poem 'founded on the affections', and Wordsworth or Dorothy might have seen such a person as the weaver, trudging under his burden on the Cumberland roads. But it is a most fortunate thing that the author resisted her feeling that 'the story would have lent itself best to metrical rather than prose fiction' – we might have had a verse tale of extreme tediousness, instead of a minor masterpiece. Her verse could not have risen to the 'feelings and emanations' of *Michael*. She particularly wished for verse for 'all that relates to the psychology of Silas', but felt that it would not allow 'an equal play of humour' – and indeed her verse would not. Moreover it must have been most inadequate to the Cass part of the story.

'The Nemesis is a very mild one' – it is a pity that it should be presented as a Nemesis at all. Godfrey married the excellent Nancy Lammeter, and looked forward to having children; but Nancy's only child, born some two years after their marriage, died in infancy. We are intended to feel that this was a punishment on Godfrey for disowning Eppie – whom he knew to be well cared for, and for whom he did as much as he dared without risking comment. God might be thought to inflict such a punishment, but the punishments of Fate have to come out of ourselves. There was nothing in Godfrey's actions to doom him to childlessness – any more than in Honoria Dedlock's in *Bleak House*. Lady Dedlock was even more guiltless of abandoning her daughter, because she did not believe her to be alive. But the long contorted plot of *Bleak House* will allow of things that shock and surprise in so well-wrought and so small as book as *Silas Marner*.

Perhaps there is some superstitious feeling behind it: '*The King shall live without an heir if that which is lost be not found.*' This is no more respectable than Godfrey's encouraging his fears 'with that superstitious impression that clings to us all, that if we expect evil very strongly it is less likely to happen' (I. viii). This impression can be rationally explained: 'If I expect the worst, it will not come upon me as an unpleasant surprise.' It is often this reasonable thought that gives birth to that 'superstitious impression'. Godfrey's childlessness is

---

[6] Haight *Letters*, III, p. 382.

required by the plot as a cause of further scenes; it should be in the book, but as an accident – and no rare or improbable accident either. The mistake is to make us feel it as the effect of his first disgraceful marriage.

As time goes on, he very much wishes to adopt Eppie, and on two occasions he tries to persuade his wife. Nancy resists, though it gives her pain to oppose him. As in the case of everyone in the book who goes through an important process of thought, her intellectual position is analysed. 'To adopt a child, because children of your own had been denied you, was to try and choose your lot in spite of Providence' (I. xvii), and it would lead to no good. 'When you saw a thing was not meant to be . . . it was a bounden duty to leave off as much as wishing for it.' Nancy's is a quiet submission to the Divine Will, as revealed to her by ordinary life – it is not an exalted renunciation like Maggie's, but all the firmer for that. 'It might seem singular that Nancy – with her religious theory pieced together out of narrow social traditions, fragments of church doctrine imperfectly understood, and girlish reasonings on her small experience – should have arrived by herself at a way of thinking so nearly akin to that of many devout people, whose beliefs are held in the shape of a system quite remote from her knowledge – singular, if we did not know that human beliefs, like all other natural growths, elude the barriers of system.'

It had never occurred to Godfrey 'that Silas would rather part with his life than with Eppie'. Though so little above them in education – and perhaps just because he was so little above them – Godfrey could not imagine deep affection to exist among the labouring people around him. 'It was only the want of adequate knowledge that could have made it possible for Godfrey deliberately to entertain an unfeeling project.' It was his tenderness for Nancy's feelings that had prevented him from telling her the truth about his relationship to Eppie, and his wish to have a child in the house and to redeem the past is wholly amiable. His fault was lack of resignation to his childlessness: 'I suppose it is the way with all men and women who reach middle age without a clear perception that life never *can* be thoroughly joyous: under the vague dulness of the grey hours, dissatisfaction seeks a definite object, and finds it in the privation of an untried good.'

The matter had not been broached between Godfrey and Nancy for four years, when the draining of the quarry – part of a farming project of Godfrey's – revealed Dunstan's skeleton, identified by his watch and seals and Godfrey's gold-handled whip. With it were Silas Marner's money bags.

The shock of this discovery moved Godfrey to confession to his wife. "Everything comes to light, Nancy, sooner or later. When God Almighty wills it our secrets are found out" (I. xvii). Nothing but a miracle could now reveal Eppie's parentage, but he is in a great state of emotion. Nancy replies: "Do you think I'd have refused to take her in, if I'd known she was yours?" He has misjudged her: but he could only have had Eppie had he owned her on the day of her mother's death, and no one knows (not even Nancy herself) if she would then have married him. Godfrey and his wife go straight to Silas's cottage to claim the girl.

First they invite her to share their home. Silas leaves Eppie to speak, and she refuses to leave him. Godfrey, possessed by his own feelings – which are good, as far as they go – has no room for the appreciation of the feelings of anyone else. He now acknowledges Eppie as his child, and claims her as her father. Even Nancy, whose 'way of thinking' was limited, felt that 'a father by blood must have a claim above that of any foster-father' (I. xviii). It appears from newspaper accounts of legal actions that many people today are not free from this superstition.

Silas now feels entitled to say that it is too late to take her from him, and Eppie says that she will never leave him, and will marry a working-man who will live with them and help her to take care of him. But we are allowed to think that Godfrey and his wife will be happier for the effort that he has made.

Nancy says to him: "My only trouble would be gone if you resigned yourself to the lot that's been given us."

"Well, perhaps it isn't too late to mend a bit there," he replies. "Though it *is* too late to mend some things, say what they will."

No eminent sinner in George Eliot's novels ever escapes scot-free, or can wholly undo the wrong he has done; there is no instance of triumphant evil. One minor sinner, however, goes unpunished, as far as we know: Silas Marner's treacherous friend, William Dane. This is because the author does not intend Silas to be righted, and she has lost interest in William Dane.

"It *is* too late to mend some things" and 'life never *can* be thoroughly joyous.' Italics are rare in George Eliot's books, and here she is emphasising her underlying view of life.

It is Dolly Winthrop who helps Silas to understand that the righteous can be forsaken. "It comes into my head as Them above has got a deal tenderer heart nor what I've got – for I can't be anyways better nor Them as made me, and if anything looks hard to me, it's because there's things I don't know on, for it's little as I know – there it is" (I. xvi). Dolly's "Them" was no heresy, 'but only her way of avoiding a presumptuous familiarity' (I. x). George Eliot did not believe in a Creator, whether merciful or no – but she was trying here, through Dolly's humble theology, to show how Silas might be brought to see that his Maker's ways were inscrutable. "For if us as know so little can see a bit o' good and rights, we may be sure as there's a good and rights bigger nor what we can know. We must trusten."

Silas replies: "There's good i' this world – I've a feeling of that now, and it makes a man feel as there's a good more nor he can see, i' spite of the trouble and the wickedness. That drawing o' the lots is dark, but the child was sent to me: there's dealings with us – there's dealings" (I. xvi).

This will do for Silas – but for the author there were no "dealings".

After the return of his gold, Silas determined to revisit Lantern Yard in the hope that something might have occurred to prove his innocence, and to question the minister about the drawing of lots. Here in Raveloe, taking part in the very different life of the parish church, he has come to look at the matter with different eyes.

Silas and Eppie reach the town, but Lantern Yard is gone; Silas can never hear if there still are people who believe him to be guilty, can never discuss the drawing of lots with the minister.

"I doubt it will be dark to the last," he says to Dolly.

"Well, yes, Master Marner," says Dolly, ". . . I doubt it may. It's the will o' them above that many things should be dark to us; but there's some things as I've never felt i' the dark about, and they're mostly what comes i' the day's work. You were hard done by that once, Master Marner, and it seems as you'll never know the rights of it, but that doesn't hinder there *being* a rights, Master Marner, for all it's dark to you and me" (I. xxi).

Silas says that since the child has come he has had "light enough to trusten by" – but in what?

After *Silas Marner* George Eliot took a new turn. It is commonly said that she had exhausted the vein of her early Warwickshire recollections, but that might not be the whole story. An author so deeply interested in the thought process of her characters must soon wish to get inside more cultivated minds than that of Silas 'in which the form and feeling have never been severed by an act of reflection'; or that of Nancy 'with her religious theory pieced together out of narrow social traditions, fragments of church doctrine imperfectly understood, and girlish reasonings on her small experience'; or that of Godfrey, equally ignorant of 'the subtle and varied pains springing from the higher sensibility that accompanies higher culture'.

George Eliot might also wish for more complicated moral cases. In *Silas Marner* she has tried to make us see a moral conflict in the mind of Godfrey Cass. But when he settles down at the end of the book as an *homme moyen sensuel* he is simply becoming content with being what he always was, and was meant by nature to be. We are asked to make too much of his 'cruel wish' for Molly's death – which he did nothing to further – and of his small prevarications.

As yet the author has not attempted much 'delineation' of the 'varieties' of human nature: she has set herself almost as a duty the task of exciting sympathy for the inarticulate. She might by now think she had fulfilled this duty, or that she had been mistaken in seeing this as a duty for the novelist.

V Romola

The first thing to be said about *Romola* has been said by nearly everyone: it is a failure. The author said that she started to write it as a young woman and ended as an old one, and to read it is not an enlivening experience. It would seem that she had come to the end of her Warwickshire material, and needed another field. She had the example of Walter Scott before her; when he had exhausted the vein that produced his border novels, he wrote mediaeval and renaissance romances. It is possible that she was directly copying him in this search for a second subject. He had begun with stories about his own country and people, often set in a period not much more than twenty-five years before his birth. George Eliot's novels had also been set in the recent past. 'As I often tell her,' wrote Lewes, 'most of the scenes and characters of her books are quite as *historical* to her personal experience as the fifteenth century in Florence.'[1] This might be so, but he was forgetting all that precious experience which is neither direct nor personal that she could possess about Warwickshire before the date of her birth, but could never gain about Florence.

The historical novel was a form more respected in the eighteen-sixties than it generally is today. George Eliot belonged to a generation that had been brought up to disapprove of novels, but made an unique exception for Scott on account of his high moral tone. Manzoni had followed with *I Promessi Sposi*, a finer work of art than Scott was capable of, and even more edifying; while Thackeray's *Esmond*, though a smaller work, is one of the most exquisite finish, and probably the most beautiful historical novel that can ever be related by a character contemporary with the story. It may have been *Romola* that

[1] Haight *Letters*, III, p. 420.

started the decline in esteem for the genre – good though its
immediate reception had been. Nothing could be more
natural as the result of so great a failure by so highly regarded
an author.

Some of the objections levelled against the historical novel
are merely inept. It is sometimes called 'escapist' – which
might or might not be a good thing (according to the sense that
is given to the foolish word). This is the last thing that it is
likely to be. The novelist generally chooses a period much more
uncomfortable than that in which he himself is living. It
would be absurd to suggest that George Eliot was 'escaping'
from Dorking in the eighteen-sixties into the far more turbulent
world of quattrocento Florence, or that (for example) Miss
H. F. M. Prescott chose the unhappy world of the Pilgrimage
of Grace as an escape from Oxfordshire in the nineteen-
fifties. Neither had any need to escape, and indeed George
Eliot's chief trouble at the time was the writing of *Romola*.
Writers often pity themselves for the 'difficult times' in which
they live, but, as times go, these, for English writers, were very
good times.

In any case, a novel is usually dated at least a little way
back in the past, because of the months it takes to write and
publish it. Novels set in the future (with rare exceptions) are a
sign that an author has nothing more to say about the present,
and perhaps nothing at all more to say.

Historical dialogue has been written in several ways. Scott
in his border novels has reproduced faithfully the dialogue of
the time – a thing only practicable when the time is not far
away. Thackerary in *Esmond* – and some other writers, notably
Rose Macaulay in *They Were Defeated* – have practised a kind
of negative archaism, that is, they deny themselves words or
references that are strikingly of their own time. Other writers
have frankly written in the language of their age, as Horace
Walpole did in *The Castle of Otranto*.

One thing, however, is always intolerable: the language of
Wardour Street. Scott, who could tell a good story even in this
abominable jargon, did much to make it popular.

George Eliot found this hideous language ready to her hand,
but she was to do even worse with it. John Blackwood wrote
to his wife: 'Her great difficulty seems to be that she, as she

describes it, hears the characters talking, and there is a weight on her mind as if Savonarola ought to be speaking Italian instead of English.'[2] Most unfortunately she lards the Wardour Street of her dialogue with Italian words and phrases. Now and then there is a technical word (e.g. *Piagnoni*, the followers of Savonarola) whose use is justified; but exclamations such as *Gnaffè* or *ebbene*, or words that have to be translated in footnotes, and can be given English equivalents (e.g. *castello*, *pievano*) are merely irritating to the reader, and useless in creating 'local colour'. If George Eliot really heard them she need not have repeated them – and it is impossible to believe that she 'heard' her people speaking the language of Wardour Street, which no one has ever spoken. Possibly she thought that she was 'translating' what she 'heard', and that jargon has been all too dear to translators.

Of local colour she has been tediously lavish. The buildings and costumes are carefully described until we feel that we are present at a fancy dress ball (perhaps in Coventry) of which the theme is Florence at the end of the fifteenth century. The background of talk is also minutely worked up, and is the result of very considerable study. But on Tito's first appearance he withdraws from a knot of talkers 'not much caring to know what was probably of little interest to any but born Florentines' (ch. ii). We do not much care either. We are reminded of many bad novels about Italy that have followed, perhaps inspired by *Romola*. Such is that by 'Joseph Emery Prank' in E. M. Forster's *A Room with a View*. 'Sunset – the sunset of Italy. Under Orcagna's Loggia – the Loggia de' Lanzi, as we sometimes call it now.' Miss Lavish (who was 'Joseph Emery Prank') despised Baedeker – but Baedeker is a better companion in Florence than herself or George Eliot.

Another great difficulty about the historical novel is its hybrid character, for some historical truth is mingled with the fiction. It is at least a more reputable form than the fictionised biography, which pretends to be truthful, and has reached absurdity as written by the corrupt following of Lytton Strachey.[3] Savonarola is a historical personage living in a

[2] ibid., p. 427.
[3] This genre has been admirably exposed by Robert Graves and Alan Hodge in *The Long Week-end* (1940), pp. 341–2.

fictionised world: we do not need authority for all his words
and thoughts and actions, but only consistency with what is
really known about him – but his presence and that of other
people who really existed creates an awkwardness in the novel.
Savonarola looms too large in a story that is not his own, though
it seems to have been his personality that first inspired this
book.

The story of Tito and Romola could have been better told
without him. Nor do the political intrigues in Florence hold
our attention much more than the complicated legal background to *Felix Holt*. It is necessary that Tito should be
treacherous, but it would have been better to confine his
treachery to individuals in whom we have some interest, and
not to direct it against men and causes not ours. People do not
care hotly for causes for very long, and treachery to them in
history is easily forgiven or explained away. E. M. Forster
was blamed by some people when he said that he hoped that,
if he had to choose, he would be brave enough to betray his
country rather than his friend. It would take more courage:
those who betray their country may end on the gallows, those
who betray their friends are frequently decorated. But it is
those who betray their friends whose infamy is eternal. The
only excuse that has ever been offered for Judas is that he acted
from nationalistic motives; it is no excuse.

The book is so full of name-dropping that one is irreverently
reminded of Beerbohm's *Savonarola Brown* – which was probably
inspired by it. It is carefully free from anachronism (one has
not heard of a single factual error of this sort discovered in it),
but it is packed with everyone of note who could have been in
Florence at the time. Tito and Romola are overwhelmed, like
guests of small account who have the misfortune to attend a
party too grand for them.

Nevertheless English historical fiction provided better
examples. Scott's discreet use of the Duke of Argyll, Queen
Caroline and Lady Suffolk in *The Heart of Midlothian* is a case
in point; they are seen through the eyes of Jeanie Deans and
are active in the promotion of her story. In the same novel the
Porteous riots provide the crowd scenes (which George Eliot
less effectively reproduced in fancy dress), and they are an
organic part of the plot. But the best use of history ever made

by a novelist is probably that made by Thackeray in *Vanity Fair*. He takes a simple and well-known course of events: Napoleon's escape from Elba, the Hundred Days, and the battle of Waterloo. We feel these events (as we should) in their effect on the lives of characters in whom we are deeply interested. For us, Napoleon has escaped in order that the funds should go down, that the Sedleys should be ruined and that old Osborne should break off the match between George and Amelia. Waterloo is fought in order that George may lie dead on the battlefield.

Romola has been divided into the Tito story and the idealised Romola fable.[4]

The Tito story is certainly intended to be realistic: it is another variation on George Eliot's favourite theme of temptation, of free will and self-determination, of the deadening of sensibility as the result of sin, and of the ineluctable consequences of past actions. This time we have no repentant sinner, like Arthur Donnithorne or Maggie, and no person like Godfrey Cass, who hardly has need of repentance. We have a black villain, with a charming face.

The germ of the story was given to the author by old General Pfuhl, in Berlin in 1855. She wrote down what he had told her under the heading *Edle Rache* (noble vengeance); we may hope this title was his, and not her own. 'A man of wealth in Rome adopted a poor boy he had found in the street. This boy turned a great villain and having previously entered the church managed by a series of arts to possess himself of a legal title to his benefactor's property, and finally ordered him to quit his own house, telling him he was no longer master. The outraged man killed the villain on the spot. He was imprisoned, tried and condemned for the murder. When in prison he refused to have a confessor. He said, "I wish to go to Hell, for *he* is there, and I want to follow out my revenge." '[5]

Tito's story required a larger world than that of the early novels, not only for the initial situation, but also for the temptations that the author wished to put in his way. Only in history could she have been cognizant of a grand enough world. If we go back far enough in history we are the equals

[4] *Critical Essays*, pp. 78ff.
[5] Haight *Biography*, p. 352.

of the highest and lowest, of conqueror and clown: and this is just, for we probably draw our blood from both of them.

Tito arrived in Florence, a poor Apulian Greek, rich only in jewels: from time to time we see him smitten in conscience, for the jewels are not his own to sell. It is not until the ninth chapter that we are told his story. He had been adopted by a scholar, Baldassare Calvo, who had lavished on him all his love. In the Archipelago they had become separated at sea. 'The galley had been taken by a Turkish vessel on its way to Delos', and there were many possibilities of Baldassare's death. But 'if now, under this mid-day sun, on some hot coast far away, a man somewhat stricken in years . . . a man who long years ago had rescued a little boy from a life of beggary, filth and cruel wrong, had treated him tenderly, and had been to him as a father – if that man were now under this summer sun toiling as a slave. . . ? If he were saying to himself: "Tito will find me. . . ?" ' If this were certain, Tito would not hesitate to seek him out.

Tito's first temptation was uncertainty whether Baldassare were still alive; his next was the difficulty and uncertainty of the enterprise that he must undertake for an end in itself uncertain. 'What, probably, would be the result if he were to quit Florence and go to Venice; get authoritative letters – yes, he knew that might be done – and set out for the Archipelago? Why, that he should be himself seized, and spend all his florins on preliminaries, and be again a destitute wanderer – with no more gems to sell.' And Tito had much at stake in Florence: love and a career. Yet if he were certain that Baldassare were living he would be bound to risk all – he did not quite admit that he was bound to make a search for his adoptive father even without certainty.

'He did not say to himself, what he was not ignorant of, that Greeks of distinction had made sacrifices, taken voyages again and again, and sought help from crowned and mitred heads for the sake of freeing relatives from slavery to the Turks. Public opinion did not regard this as exceptional virtue.'

Public opinion is mean – it is hard on people whose bare duty requires heroism in the performance, chary of praise when it is performed and heavy with blame if it is neglected, and unsparing towards those who have done evil under coercion.

The public is not so brave and good and nice as it thinks itself – while it judges other people by the counsels of perfection. Tito's Florentine friends, however, were entitled by their personal integrity to take the highest stand.

Only love could have been a motive power so strong that Tito would, under its influence, forget to feel ill-used by destiny; gratitude was not enough, and Tito was getting tired of the ageing and exacting Baldassare. There is no hint that there had been a homosexual relation between them, and it is improbable that George Eliot intended it. Nevertheless it seems necessary to explain the passion for revenge; it may have been behind the original story told by General Pfuhl – and in reading *Romola* we sometimes think of Antonio in *Twelfth Night,* or the other Antonio in *The Merchant of Venice,* or of Balzac's Vautrin and Lucien de Rubempré. George Eliot may very well have been influenced by stories in which homosexuality is patent or implied, so that the suggestion of it here is (I hope) not impertinent as such suggestions usually are. It is nearly always grossly impertinent criticism to assert that one knows more about a character than its author, or even to say that one has discovered what he did not choose to reveal (e.g. the specu- lations about the 'impotence' of Othello, or of Casaubon in *Middlemarch* – though, as we shall see, I think it is implied that the latter was sterile). A character only exists insofar as he is revealed, his *esse* is *percipi.* But reference to a source or an influence may be legitimate, if used with caution. Moreover, like Ladislaw in *Middlemarch,* Tito had a considerable feminine charm. 'If he declined some labour – why, he flung himself down with such a charming, half-smiling, half-pleading air, that the pleasure of looking at him made amends to one who had watched his growth with a sense of claim and possession.'

Until he had realised the money for the jewels, Tito had hedged about the fate of Baldassare. The moment he applied the money to his own purposes 'he had made it impossible that he should not from henceforth desire it to be the truth that his father was dead'. The analysis that follows is perhaps the best thing of its kind in all George Eliot's work: 'Under every guilty secret there is hidden a brood of guilty desires, whose un- wholesome infecting life is cherished by the darkness. The contaminating effect of deeds often lies less in the commission

than in the consequent adjustment of our desires – the enlistment
of our self-interest on the side of falsity . . . Besides . . . the ideas
which had previously been scattered and interrupted had now
concentrated themselves; the little rills of selfishness had united
and made a channel, so that they could never again meet with
the same resistance. Hitherto Tito had left in vague indecision
the question whether, with the means in his power, he would
return and ascertain his father's fate; he had now made a
definite excuse to himself for not taking that course . . .'

Almost immediately afterwards he is identified (because he
is wearing Baldassare's ring) by Romola's brother who had
run away to become a Dominican. Fra Luca gives him a note
from Baldassare: "I think they are going to take me to Antioch."
His duty is clear: he must search for his adoptive father –
though it will still be with uncertainty. He can repossess himself
of his florins, now put out on loan; it is still possible for him to
explain away his previous inaction – but he has now gone too
far towards deadening his conscience. Public opinion will force
him to act if the friar tells other people about the message –
but the friar is dying, and Tito keeps it to himself. He has the
unpleasant and not uncommon notion that pleasure is the
due of his youth – moreover he lacks 'that awe of the Divine
Nemesis which was felt by religious pagans, and . . . is still felt
by the mass of mankind, simply as a vague fear of anything
which is called wrongdoing' (ch. xi). He receives a bad shock
when he learns that Fra Luca is Romola's brother, and fears
that he will be exposed to her, after which she must inevitably
turn against him. But the friar dies after communicating a
vision to her, and without telling his story. Nevertheless Tito,
who cared so much for men's good opinion (and still had seeds
of goodness in himself) began to regret that he had shirked his
obligations.

'But our deeds are like children that are born to us; they live
and act apart from our own will. Nay, children may be
strangled, but deeds never: they have an indestructible life in
and out of our consciousness; and that dreadful vitality of deeds
was pressing hard on Tito for the first time' (ch. xvi). Yet
gradually he came to feel that fortune had brought him immunity: 'He was not aware that that very delight in immunity
which prompted resolutions not to entangle himself again, was

deadening the sensibilities which alone could save him from
entanglement' (ch. xviii).

Admirable as such passages are, it will not do to regard
Romola merely as a collection of moral essays or aphorisms.
It is the story (among other things) of one who 'tried to slip
away from everything that was unpleasant' (Epilogue). Its
moral is also *nemo repente fit turpissimus*, which requires a story
drawn out at some length. Tito is a woman-novelist's young
man, but less uninteresting than Stephen Guest or such bores
as Felix Holt and Daniel Deronda; and his final worthlessness
is at least credible as the final worthiness of Ladislaw in
Middlemarch is not.

He is, perhaps, the only character who profits by the fancy
dress atmosphere of *Romola*. Characters in fiction, who cannot
be seen, lose the advantage of such physical beauty as may be
theirs. An author will try to do what he can for them, apart
from indirectly showing the effect of their beauty on other
people – as Hetty's and Rosamond's are shown. He may try to
connect them in the reader's mind with some work of art that
he can (even if only vaguely) represent in his mind's eye: thus
Proust's Odette is a Botticelli, and Henry James's Milly Theale
is a Bronzino. Tito is a handsome young Florentine out of an
indistinctly imagined crowd scene in a picture by Benozzo
Gozzoli, or some other painter of the time.

Baldassare, when he makes his appearance as an avenger,
forfeits the sympathy with which the reader has previously
regarded him. He is an escaped prisoner; unlike Vautrin or
Magwitch he is no criminal, but a most unfortunate man;
and his young protegé has been basely ungrateful. But he is as
hideous as a devil, and has become a force of evil – false as
Tito is, we now prefer him to the man whom he has wronged,
for at least what he desires from life would be good – if he
could possess it honourably, while Baldassare has nothing good
in his heart at all.

' "*Some madman surely*," said Tito.

'He hardly knew how the words had come to his lips:
there are moments when our passions speak and decide for us,
and we seem to stand by and wonder' (ch. xxii).

Later he was to think with bitterness how easily he could have
made Baldassare believe that he had been convinced of his

death; but that would have required perfect self-command at their sudden meeting – and he was perhaps not yet bad enough to have self-command without a clear conscience. 'Tito was experiencing that inexorable law of human souls, that we prepare ourselves for sudden deeds by the reiterated choice of good and evil that gradually determines character' (ch. xxiii). It is therefore not unjust to judge a man by his conduct in an emergency – his whole life has prepared it.

There was still one resource open to him, Confession. But 'the repentance that cuts off all moorings to evil, demands something more than selfish fear. He had no sense that there was strength and safety in truth; the only strength he trusted to lay in his ingenuity and dissimulation.' And yet Tito is not wholly evil, he is not at all cruel, and he would far prefer that Baldassare should not suffer.

Baldassare's hatred grows. Everything feeds it, even the violent preaching of Savonarola – and above all the fear (which events fully justify) that he will not be able to prove his identity as a scholar and no madman. His uncertain memory is, as a plot contrivance, to be ranked with Silas Marner's epilepsy and Christian's opium sleep – a weakness that the author would have done well to avoid.

Tito is deprived of his last chance of restitution. 'A few steps, and he might be face to face with his father, with no witness by; he might seek forgiveness and reconciliation' (ch. xxiv). Baldassare leaps at him with a dagger, which breaks against the chain mail that he is wearing. "*Padre mio!*" he says. "I came to ask your forgiveness . . . I was taken by surprise that morning. I wish to be a son to you again. I wish to make the rest of your life happy, that you may forget what you have suffered."

That Baldassare should not forgive him in a hurry, or ever quite completely, need surprise no one: but the violence of his hatred and his lust for revenge forbids us to consider him any more as a moral agent – and it is surprising that George Eliot, with her belief in Christian morality, is not louder in his condemnation. 'Tito felt he had no choice now: he must defy Baldassare as a mad, imbecile old man.' The Tito-Baldassare story, degenerated into a struggle between two evil forces, is no longer of moral interest. Nevertheless the collapse of Tito's character has been one of the finest of all George Eliot's moral stories, and it is a pity that it is embedded in a novel that so little attracts the reader as *Romola*.

An appendage to the Tito story is that of Tessa. This little village girl, married to Tito in a mock ceremony during a fête, really believes herself to be his wife. At first he means to disillusion her, but finally lives with her as a largely absentee husband, and she bears him two charming children. His tenderness in this irregular relationship is, strangely, the best thing about his life in Florence. Tessa and her children end up as part of Romola's little court, as attendant figures grouped round a Madonna.

Mr John Bayley has made an amusing and interesting suggestion.[6] 'It is usually taken for granted that James's *Portrait of a Lady* owes much to the *Middlemarch* situation [does he not mean *Daniel Deronda*?] but in fact it possibly owes even more to the triangular pattern of *Romola*, with Tessa oddly but effectively transmuted into Madame Merle.' He writes: 'Tito is as much as home in Tessa's placidity as James's Gilbert Osmond is in Madame Merle's worldliness. Both are undone by the supposition that their wives will acquiesce in the limits which enable them to be good to themselves and others.' Nevertheless, the comfort that Osmond finds in Madame Merle is limited, and she is an unscrupulous conspirator, quite unlike the innocent Tessa. Osmond is, like Grandcourt, essentially a cold fish – and very unlike Tito. And Tessa would hardly have 'acquiesced' in Tito's wickedness had she been aware of it.

Romola is always seen as an exaggeratedly noble character. Tito comes to work for her father, Bardo. 'He felt himself strangely in subjection to Romola with that majestic simplicity of hers; he felt for the first time, without defining it to himself, that loving awe in the presence of noble womanhood, which is perhaps something like the worship paid of old to a great nature-goddess, who was not all-knowing, but whose life and power were something deeper and more primordial than knowledge' (ch. ix). Nearly every time she makes an appearance everyone regards her with a reverence due among women only to the Blessed Virgin. It is only Savonarola who tries to put

[6] *Critical Essays*, p. 213.

her in her place, but we are so much annoyed by his injustice that she is rather exalted by it than otherwise.

Readers have seen a kind of wish-fulfilment or self-glorification in this Madonna figure; it would be fairer to call her an ideal after which the author felt bound to strive, and by whose standard she rebuked herself. 'You are right in saying Romola is ideal,' she wrote to a friend. 'I feel it acutely in the reproof my own soul is constantly getting from the image it has made. My own books scourge me.'[7]

Suspicion soon begins to enter into Romola's marriage with Tito. After the appearance of Baldassare he begins to wear chain mail, and he will not tell her why. He becomes colder towards her, feeling 'a certain repulsion towards a woman from whose mind he was in danger' (ch. xxvi). So Casaubon, in his different way, was to fear the mind of Dorothea.

In Piero di Cosimo's workshop she sees a sketch of Tito, with an expression of terror. ' "It means nothing," she tried to reassure herself. "It was a mere coincidence. Shall I ask Tito about it?" Her mind said at last, "No: I will not question him about anything he did not tell me spontaneously. It is an offence against the trust I owe him." Her heart said, "I dare not ask him." There was a terrible flaw in the trust: she was afraid of any hasty movement, as men are who hold something precious and want to believe that it is not broken.'

Romola has been living for the conservation of her father's name, and for the books and antiquities of his collection that are to make it immortal. Tito sells them. ' "You are a treacherous man!" she said. "Have you robbed someone else who is *not* dead? Is that the reason that you wear armour?" ' (ch. xxviii). It can hardly be wondered at that Tito, though his serious love is for Romola, finds comfort in the cosiness of the unquestioning Tessa. 'Poor Romola, with all her self-sacrificing effort, was really helping to harden Tito's nature by chilling it with a positive dislike which had beforehand seemed impossible in him; but Tessa kept open the fountains of kindness.' This is valuable criticism of the enskyed and sainted Romola. She is

> too greatly good
> For human nature's daily food.

---

[7] Haight *Letters*, IV, pp. 103–4.

The unyieldingness of those whom he has wronged does much to earn for Tito the sympathy of which he is so badly in need.

Romola, profiting by an absence of his, decides on flight. She has no religious convictions about the sanctity of marriage. 'She was going to solve the problem in a way that seemed to her very simple. Her mind had never yet bowed to any obligation apart from personal love and reverence; she had no keen sense of any other human relations, and all she had to obey now was the instinct to sever herself from the man she loved no longer' (ch. xxvii). She meant to go in a pilgrim's garb to a learned woman in Venice, and to find a way of supporting herself.

Savonarola stops Romola on the way, and it is remarkable that his pleading with her has not more often been attacked for the impertinence that it was. First he says that he has a command from God to stop her: she has little belief in God, and has already a very reasonable distrust for his self-styled messengers. Then he tells her that she is forsaking her duties as a Florentine woman and a wife. But she does not recognise matrimony as a sacrament, and the merely human pledge involved would not be sufficient to hold her bound to Tito – who, in any case, no longer much wanted her. Savonarola tells her to live for Florence, but there can be no reason why she should feel tied to her birthplace when a possibly useful life awaits her in Venice. Even if Florence were already suffering – and it was two years later that famine and disease were to come – Romola who had no gifts or training for social work might quite legitimately go away. And she has no reason to believe (and by the end of the book no one can much believe) in "the great work by which Florence is to be regenerated and the world made holy" (ch. xl). Nor is there any sacrilege in adopting the garb of a pilgrim, which is no more than semi-religious. Romola gives way to this impertinent appeal. Had she been a religious woman she might probably have resisted it, for she would have recognised that only human magnetism gave it force.

She went back to what she supposed to be her duty. She had not forsaken Tito, but 'there is a forsaking which still sits at the same board and lies on the same couch with the forsaken soul,

withering it the more by unloving proximity' (ch. lxxiv) – so
Mrs Bulstrode in *Middlemarch* would not forsake her husband.
'Tito and Romola never jarred, never remonstrated with each
other. They were too hopelessly alienated in their inner life
even to have that contest which is an effort towards agreement' (ch. xl). They lived as Gwendolen and Grandcourt were
later to live. When Romola learned about Tessa she was far
from jealous; on the contrary she was seized with the hope that
Tessa was Tito's legal wife, and that her own marriage was
invalid. Baldassare has one moment when he is human and
moving in his self-revelation to Romola: "Ah! You would
have been my daughter!" (ch. liii).

Her second great interview with Savonarola reverses the
effect of the first. She has gone to plead for the life of a condemned Medicean, her godfather, a noble old man, Bernardo
del Nero.

Savonarola's reply is repellent: "The cause of freedom,
which is the cause of God's kingdom on earth, is often most
injured by the enemies who carry within them the power of
certain human virtues" (ch. lix).

Romola is angry and in despair. Savonarola then makes the
appeal of a public man to a private conscience.

"Be thankful, my daughter, if your own soul has been spared
perplexity; and judge not those to whom a harder lot has been
given. *You* see one ground of action in this matter. I see many.
I have to choose that which will further the work entrusted to
me. The end I see is one to which minor respects must be
sacrificed. The death of five men – were they less guilty than
these – is a light matter against the withstanding of the vicious
tyrannies which stifle the life of Italy, and foster the corruption
of the Church; a light matter weighed against the furthering of
God's kingdom on earth, the end for which I live and am
willing myself to die." This is Pilate's argument, in disguise.

The beginning of this speech might touch a private conscience,
unburdened with the "harder lot", and we are told that 'under
any other circumstances' Romola would have been sensitive to
it – but in her strong antagonism 'that which he called
perplexity seemed to her sophistry and doubleness'. She
answers bitterly: "Take care father, lest your enemies have
some reason when they say, that in your visions of what will

further God's kingdom, you see only what will strengthen your own party."

' "And that is true!" said Savonarola . . . "the cause of my party *is* the cause of God's kingdom."

' "I do not believe it!" said Romola . . . "God's kingdom is something wider – else – let me stand outside it with the beings that I love." '

This is the climax of Romola's conscience, now freed from Savonarola's influence. It is also George Eliot's fullest expression of her repudiation of politics and the 'public' conscience.

Romola now makes a second flight. It might be thought that having lived all this time as a *Piagnone* she might have come more fully to believe in Savonarola's earlier arguments, and that life and thought would have given confirmation to what had only been enforced on her by his personal magnetism. The sacrament of matrimony must now have a meaning for her, and she had a place in Florence and work there, as she had not before. What has gone is the power that Savonarola had over her; we now think less of her because of her return and her present flight.

'A new rebellion had risen within her, a new despair . . . What force was there to create for her that supremely hallowed motive which men call duty, but which can have no inward constraining influence save through some form of believing love?' (ch. lxi). She had lost faith in matrimony more deeply with her deeper loss of faith in Tito, and 'the sense of a confusion in human things' replaced her feeling of duty to others. Above all, she had lost faith in Savonarola, who had sent her back to both. 'No one who has ever known what it is to lose faith in a fellow-man whom he has profoundly loved and reverenced, will lightly say that the shock can leave the faith in the Invisible Goodness unshaken.' 'Lightly', perhaps not, but seriously it may be said – and perhaps we may dare to add that this is one of George Eliot's specifically feminine reactions. Moreover Romola has not suffered the worst at Savonarola's hands; he has in no way betrayed her. But as far as Florence is concerned, Romola is fully entitled now to think first of herself and her own sorrows, for few have given them a thought.

Near 'the little fishing village of Viareggio' she gets into a boat (for which she scrupulously leaves the money behind) and lets herself drift out to sea. Next day she wakes in a little creek, where she finds a village stricken with pestilence, apparently brought there by Jewish exiles.

Then follows the apotheosis of Romola, 'the lady from over the sea', the almost thaumaturgic benefactress. For her this is a return out of a dream world into a real world. In famine-stricken Florence she had been glad to live, though in love with death, because she could lighten the sorrow of others; now she thinks only of lightening sorrow. Finally she comes to feel that her second flight had no more justification than that from which Savonarola had turned her back. There might still be duties for her towards Tito and towards Florence (ch. lxix).

Many people have been amused that Romola should seek out Tito's mistress Tessa, and set up house with her and her two children – and yet it seems right to leave her in a happy domestic setting, with more company than her foolish old cousin, Monna Brigida. So much of the sweetness of George Eliot's own life was due to her happy relations with Lewes's sons; perhaps she wished to give Romola a similar consolation.

Romola had one great fault, the fault to which Mr Darcy owned in *Pride and Prejudice*.

'My temper would perhaps be called resentful. My good opinion once lost is lost for ever.'

Elizabeth justly thought 'implacable resentment' a terrible fault. One is uncomfortably uncertain how far George Eliot would agree – and whether she did not see something 'noble' about Baldassare's vengeance.

The story of Dino leaves us uncomfortable. Romola's father Bardo, a blind collector and (there are some indications) a barren scholar, considers that his son, Dino, has committed an intolerable act of desertion in leaving him and the life of scholarship to join the Dominican order as Fra Luca. "My son, whom I had brought up to replenish my ripe learning with young enterprise, left me and all liberal pursuits that he might lash himself and howl at midnight with besotted friars" (ch. v). Even a cross and disappointed old man like Bardo, living in Florence in the fifteenth century, could hardly speak as a Victorian protestant businessman might have spoken, if his son had forsaken the family firm to follow an eccentric like Father Ignatius. And Romola, though the agnostic daughter of a

humanistic father, must have been aware of religious vocation
as a not uncommon phenomenon of the time. She might
reasonably regret Dino's action, but she could hardly have
regarded it as a selfish and treacherous betrayal. Nevertheless,
when she was summoned to her brother's death-bed: 'There was
an unconquerable repulsion for her in that monkish aspect:
it seemed to her the brand of the dastardly undutifulness which
had left her father desolate – of the grovelling supersition which
could give such undutifulness the stamp of piety . . . she had no
ideas that could render her brother's course an object of any
other feeling than incurious, indignant contempt . . .' (ch. xv).
Dino had a message for her, and she could only imagine that it
must be a message of repentance for her father. She is punished
for this lack of sympathy; a little closer contact with Dino and
she would have learned the story of Tito and Baldassare. All
she hears (and with some impatience) is a vision about her
future unhappy marriage.

In spite of George Eliot's 'deep personal sympathies with the
old reforming priest',[8] it is impossible not to feel that
Savonarola's presence is unnecessary to the more living part of
the book, and that therefore it would have been better without
him. He is however an interesting example of the 'public'
conscience, and raises the question whether political life is
compatible not only with the counsels of perfection, but even
with 'la morale des gens honnêtes', and the answer appears to
be in the negative. There have been sainted popes and kings,
but perhaps no sainted statesman except Sir Thomas More –
and he died a martyr. Savonarola had the disadvantage of
martyrdom without the credit of sainthood.

[8] Haight *Letters*, III, p. 420.

VI   Felix Holt

Felix Holt is a new beginning, and a different kind of failure. Neither this book nor *Romola* invites others than students to a complete re-reading, though in *Felix Holt* it is easier to look back and pick out the good part – that concerned with Mrs Transome. In a sense this is a greater condemnation of the whole: *Romola* has for its main theme the moral disintegration of Tito, and one can more or less ignore the introduction of Savonarola as Romola's spiritual director – it is more a question of rejecting the bad parts (as later in *Daniel Deronda*) than in picking out what is good. Nevertheless, *Felix Holt* contains the finest work that George Eliot had yet done, and it has the advantage of being written in a language in which there is no place for the Wardour Street of *Romola*, and where the writer has not yet developed the flatulent symbolism of *Middlemarch*.

It has been argued with force that the first germ of the story lay in the relations of Mrs Transome, the lawyer Jermyn and their natural son, Harold.[1] On the other hand, it has also been maintained with some reason that the title indicates George Eliot's intention to write a book about Radicalism[2] and the opening of the novel appears to announce this. The two contentions are probably correct – there is no difficulty in reconciling them. George Eliot surely had both themes in her mind before she started on the book, and it matters little which first occurred to her. Unfortunately it was not so easy for her to reconcile them.

The book opens with a splendid picture of the Midlands just after the passing of the Reform Bill of 1832. Then we arrive at Treby, a newly enfranchised borough, on which two characters are converging: they are Felix Holt, the quack doctor's son, come from his studies, and Harold Transome, the squire's

[1] Introduction to Penguin edition, by Peter Coveney.
[2] *Critical Essays*, p. 99ff.

putative son, come from making money in the Levant. 'There could hardly have been a lot less like Harold Transome's than this of the quack doctor's son, except in the superficial facts that each called himself a Radical, that he was the only son of his mother, and that he had lately returned to his home with ideas and resolves not a little disturbing to that mother's mind' (ch. 3).

Harold's Radicalism is cynical and opportunist, Felix Holt's is idealistic – their lives run almost parallel, and hardly ever meet.[3] We may or may not see their opposition as 'the core of the novel' – but it appears to have been intended to be just that. Possibly we may agree with the critic who said that George Eliot seems to have promised to write a novel that she did not write – one on Radicalism. Why she did not write it must be a matter for conjecture – did Mrs Transome steal the story, or did Felix seem too unreal?

Mrs Hardy[4] finds the 'narrative irony' resulting from the opposition between the two 'radicals' to be one of the chief interests in the book. 'The irony culminates in Harold's loss of Esther and his gain of the estate, both brought about by Felix's influence. The parallel is found in Felix's imprisonment, in its turn brought about by Harold.' This may, perhaps, be what George Eliot intended, but it is hardly an account of what she achieved. A preference for Felix did determine Esther to choose him and his world, but it is straining the story very far to make Harold responsible for Felix's imprisonment.

Unfortunately the main tie between the two stories is the young woman, Esther Lyon. She is more a feeble *ficelle* than a heroine, and a *ficelle* entangled in a very complicated and knotty confusion.

Of all the dead matter in George Eliot's novels, the most tiresome is the business of the Transome estate. Trollope would have made it clear, and perhaps exciting; Dickens would have enwrapped it in obscure villainy. George Eliot draws the minimum of interest from the maximum of obscurity. No one

---

[3] 'The reviewer in *The English Review*, for October 1866, complained that "the story has the defect of running in two parallel lines, with only an occasional and arbitrary connexion" ' ibid., p. 90.

[4] ibid., p. 93.

is likely to understand the case at a first reading, and its complication is one of the main reasons that will deter readers from a second attempt.

The coachman of the *Introduction* points out Transome Court as 'a place there had been a fine sight of lawsuits about'. He mentions that the present owners, distant connexions of the name of Durfey, have taken the name Transome because they got the estate through some bargain with the heir of the Transomes, but that the Durfey's claim has often been disputed.

When Harold Transome arrives home from the East, he finds that the family has been impoverished by lawsuits. Later they are called 'ugly lawsuits' (ch. 2) – which would seem to imply either that they had been dangerous to the Transomes' claims, or that they had been unfairly fought, or both. It is known to the upper servants at Treby Manor (the other great house of the neighbourhood) that a 'scamp' called Henry Scaddon had claimed to be the heir.

George Eliot had appealed to Frederic Harrison for legal advice.

'It is required to know the longest possible term of years for the existence of the following conditions:
1. That an estate, for lack of a direct heir, should have come into the possession of A (or of a series A, A′, A″ – if that were admissible).
2. That subsequently a claim should have been set up by B, on a valid plea of nearer kinship. [Note – the plea is valid, but not the claim.]
3. That B should have failed in his suit from inability to prove his identity, over which certain circumstances (already fixed) should have cast a doubt, and should have died soon after.
4. That B's daughter, being an infant at the time of his death, should have come to years of discretion and have a legal claim to the estate.'[5]

George Eliot, then, had from the beginning the idea of producing the girl Esther as the heir. She wished for time in

[5] Haight *Letters*, IV, p. 216.

which the complications might develop, and that she should not be barred by any statute of limitations by which sixty years or so of ownership constitute an inalienable right to an estate.

With Harrison's aid a complex but possible pattern was devised. This is stated (ch. 29) when Johnson, the partner – accomplice of the Transome lawyer, Jermyn – has sorted out the facts.

John Justus Transome, some 'hundred years ago', had settled the estate, entailing it on his son Thomas and his heirs-male, with remainder to his distant connections the Bycliffes 'in fee'. This entail could only be broken by John Justus and Thomas acting in conjunction. Thomas, who was a prodigal, had without his father's knowledge or consent sold his own rights and those of his heirs to a lawyer-cousin, Durfey. Durfey, taking the name and arms of Transome, had therefore legally succeeded John Justus. He had only the 'base fee' created by Thomas – but it had been worth buying, for Thomas had several children and there was no need to expect his line to die out. He tried to represent his claim as absolute, but the Bycliffes (whose interest he had not bought) 'were the "remainder-men" who might fairly oust the Durfey-Transomes if ever the issue of the prodigal Thomas went clean out of existence and ceased to represent a right which he had bargained away from them'.

This highly complicated legal situation (with which equity has nothing to do) is further confused by mistaken identity, and by the fact that, for a large part of the story, no one person knows more than a fragment of the case.

1. Matthew Jermyn, the Transome family lawyer (and in fact the father of Harold Transome), has exploited his position by obtaining large annuities on the estate, held in the name of his factotum, Johnson. Mrs Transome, during the years of her administration of the estate, was too much afraid to intervene. During these years a Bycliffe heir presented himself. Maurice Christian Bycliffe had served against France with the Hanoverian army in the Napoleonic wars. He found himself fellow-prisoner with a ne'er-do-well, one Henry Scaddon. Scaddon, a non-combatant, had an earlier opportunity of returning to England, and good reasons for not availing himself of it: he exchanged identities with his fellow-prisoner. Thus Maurice

Christian Bycliffe appeared in England under Scaddon's name; Jermyn managed to have him thrown into prison as Scaddon, and there he died (1811). It was supposed that he was the last of the Bycliffes, and that the Durfey-Transomes were now firmly established.

During the Bycliffe case an odd character, Tommy Trounsem, revealed himself as the last representative of Thomas Transome's line. As long as he lived the Durfey-Transomes had a valid right to the estate, even if there were to be a Bycliffe heir. Jermyn keeps this information to himself.

2. John Johnson, Jermyn's factotum, discovers this fact when Tommy Trounsem is old and down-at-heel. Tommy was trampled to death in the Treby riot (ch. 33), and this ended the Durfey-Transomes' right to the property, should there be a Bycliffe heir.

3. Henry Scaddon (alias Maurice Christian) has retained a portion of the name which he got by exchange with Bycliffe – whose last name, one would imagine, might draw too much attention. He escaped from prison, and was believed to have been drowned. In due course he came to England, and became courier to the Debarry family at Treby Manor, the principal family in the neighbourhood. He, of course, knew that Bycliffe had been what he claimed to be; he was also aware of Tommy Trounsem's position, for the old man revealed it to him.

4. Rufus Lyon is the dissenting minister in Treby. He had taken pity on a poor French woman with a baby. She said that she had escaped from France to rejoin her husband, and that she had been informed of his death soon after her arrival in England. The only possessions she had been able to preserve were her marriage certificate and a few other papers, and a locket containing her husband's hair 'and bearing his baptismal name'. She said that a similar locket, with her hair and inscribed with her name hung on his watch chain. Eventually Rufus Lyon married her, and after her death brought up her daughter as his own, in ignorance of her parentage. He was of course aware that her father was Maurice Christian Bycliffe, but the name meant nothing to him, and he had no idea that she was heiress in remainder to the Transome estates.

The machinery for the discovery of the missing heir creaks with impossibilities. After church one sunday morning Philip

Debarry, the heir of Treby, remained to luncheon at the rectory with his uncle Augustus, to consult him about some papers; inadvertently he left them behind. On coming home he was aware of this, and promptly despatched his courier, Maurice Christian, with a note to his uncle asking him to seal up the pocket-book and return it by the bearer. Christian was a sufferer from 'nervous pains', which he was careful to conceal, as well as his practice of relieving them by opium. On his way back from the rectory he fell into a deep opium sleep.

He was very much disliked by his fellow-servants on account of his superior airs. Scales, the butler, found him sleeping, cut off one of his coat tails and threw it at some distance. In the coat tail, naturally enough, was Philip Debarry's pocket-book. It was far less natural that Christian should be carrying about with him some relics of that Maurice Christian Bycliffe with whom he had long ago exchanged identity (ch. 12).

Felix Holt happened to pass by and find a leather pocket-book and the other objects. Out of inverted snobbery he had a foolish dislike of approaching the family at Treby Manor and decided to leave everything in the hands of Rufus Lyon, asking him to effect the restitution. "I've had the ill-luck to be the finder of these things in the Debarrys' Park. Most likely they belong to one of the family at the Manor, or to some grandee who is staying there. I hate having anything to do with such people. They'll think me a poor rascal, and offer me money. You are a known man, and I thought you would be kind enough to relieve me by taking charge of these things, and writing to Debarry, not mentioning me, and asking him to send someone for them." Mr Lyon does not rebuke Felix for his nasty pride – shown by the vulgar sneering word "grandee" – but it will be seen for what it is worth when we compare it with the exquisite sensibility and good manners of Philip Debarry.

The minister is deeply moved by seeing a name on the locket, of course that of Annette. At first he fears that Christian will turn out to be Esther's father (he had in the beginning suspected that Annette had been abandoned by her husband). He is partially reassured by his examination of the courier; he seeks further information from Jermyn (ch. 18), who is able to inform him that the courier is not Maurice Christian Bycliffe.

Christian himself, having noticed a remarkable likeness

between Esther and Bycliffe, and having seen the minister's emotion on his meeting with him, seeks him out. He obtains the admission that Esther is Bycliffe's daughter, and binds Rufus Lyon to silence about their conversation by telling him that Jermyn is likely to do all he can to stifle Esther's claim. Later he learns that only Tommy Trounsem's life stands between her and the estate.

On the nomination-day for the Treby election, Christian learns of Johnson's presence in the town, and pools his information with him.

Meanwhile Jermyn, now possessed of the same information, attempts to use it to blackmail Harold Transome into withdrawing his action against him for malversation of the family property. He tells him that the death of Tommy Trounsem now renders the Bycliffe claim valid, and that as soon as "the true claimant is made aware of his right" Harold must lose the estate.

The new claimant has been 'brought up in an inferior station'. "There is no harm in leaving him in ignorance. The question is a purely legal one." Jermyn claims that he alone is in possession of the evidence, which he can nullify, or make to tell with certainty against Harold and old Mr Transome. Harold asks for time to think it over (ch. 35).

Harold is an honest if not a morbidly scrupulous man. 'In ordinary cases a shorter possession than Harold's family had enjoyed was allowed by the law to constitute an indefeasible right.' It would be a great misfortune to the Transomes to be deprived of their property by a quirk of the law, and its acquisition by the missing heir would be something like winning a great sum in a lottery. Harold would have no objection to fighting the case and taking what the law gave him, were he successful. But he had a moral objection to 'the secret nullification of a just claim', and a fastidious dislike for 'what looked like complicity with Jermyn'. If he felt that the law was an ass for giving him so much trouble (and he never said so) no one could blame him.

Jermyn, however, is mistaken in thinking that he alone is in possession of the evidence. Christian calls upon Harold in the hope of selling his information – which is more complete, as he reveals Esther Lyon as the heiress. Harold is now resolved on an

honourable course – he may come to a compromise with
Esther, to avoid litigation, or perhaps unite their interests by
marrying her. Mrs Transome pleads in vain for the stopping
of Chancery proceedings against Jermyn, her former lover;
she is obliged to yield to Harold's suggestion that Esther should
be invited to Transome Court as a guest.

The legal machinery, impossible to follow on a first reading,
has here been set out in detail to save the reader trouble, and to
allow him direct access to the more significant parts of the
novel. This machinery has been set up to give Esther a choice
between two worlds, not unlike that offered to Eppie in *Silas
Marner*. If her final choice were to remain with her step-
father she might be applauded, though her tie to Rufus Lyon is
far less close than that of Eppie to Silas. But there is also the
choice between two lovers: 'Felix Holt, the Radical' and
Harold Transome, another sort of radical. Neither of them is
likely to be a perfect husband: the idealistic radicalism of
Felix may be morally superior to the cynical opportunism of
Harold, but would be just as tiresome in everyday life. Her
choice is sometimes represented as one between Right and
Wrong, and she is said to reject the dead world of Transome
Court (emphasised by so many metaphors) for life outside.
But the life outside does not seem of great importance, and she
might have brought life to Transome Court. Her choice is
right, but is the choice of Fanny Price who honestly refused a
man she did not love because she was in love with another
(and with far less prospect of success than Esther) – otherwise
we might agree with Lady Bertram that 'it is every young
woman's duty to accept such a very unexceptionable offer'.
The reader – who probably cares nothing about the three
principals – may well regret that Esther should not find it
possible to go as a daughter-in-law to Mrs Transome, to whom
she would have been a blessing.

Esther's step-father (whom she believes to be her father) is
the Congregational minister Rufus Lyon. One must agree with
Dr Leavis that he is a bore, and one would like to agree that he
is 'incredible'. His extremely annoying speeches occupy a
considerable part of the book. In another way, Felix's mother,
Mrs Holt, who is a member of his congregation, is equally
boring, and only too easily credible. The fourth chapter, which

shows these two together, seems to be an imitation of one of the worst faults of Scott, his attempt to bring humour out of endless repetition.

‘ "I lack grace to deal with these weak sisters," said the minister, again thinking aloud and walking. "Their needs lie too much out of the track of my meditations, and take me often unwares. Mistress Holt is another who darkens counsel by words without knowledge, and angers the reason of the natural man. Lord, give me patience. My sins were heavier to bear than this woman's folly . . ." '

The natural reader, under no obligation of charity to bear with Mrs Holt, may well throw down the book without praying for patience. When she comes in she complains interminably about her son. Felix is ruining her by denouncing the sale of a quack medicine, Holt's cancer cure, the invention of his late father; he has thrown up his medical studies and become a journeyman watchmaker.

It was in this dreary world that Esther lived, and it was only for the last two years that she had been there as a permanent inmate. Rufus Lyon had sent her away to a French protestant school, naively imagining that she might have inherited a gift for her mother's language. Afterwards she had occupied situations as governess in families where she acquired a refinement that seemed almost shocking to the dissenting world of Treby. 'She was not contented with her life: she seemed to herself to be surrounded with ignoble, uninteresting conditions, from which there was no issue' (ch. 6). Possibly too much influence is ascribed to her gentle blood (of which she was ignorant), though some of her physical elegance may be attributed to it; but her education has been that of a lady, and she is greatly superior in manners to all the Trebeian middle class.

Felix Holt, while apprenticed to a country apothecary, learned enough of pharmacology to be convinced that his father's patent medicines were worse than useless: "I know that the Cathartic Pills are a drastic compound which may be as bad as poison to half the people who swallow them; that the Elixir is an absurd farrago of a dozen incompatible things; and that the Cancer Cure might as well be bottled dish-water" (ch. 5). Felix proposes to maintain his mother by his work in watch and clock cleaning, and by teaching small boys.

From his first appearance he is unbearably pompous and priggish. When Mr Lyon suggests that he might do better for himself, he exclaims: "I'll take no employment that obliges me to prop up my chin with a high cravat, and wear straps, and pass the livelong day with a set of fellows who spend their spare money on shirt-pins . . . I mean to stick to the class I belong to – people who don't follow the fashions." But he does not speak like people who belong to the artisan class, or to any class whatever:

"O yes, your ringed and scented men of the people! – I won't be one of them. Let a man once trouble himself with a satin stock, and he'll get new wants and new motives. Metamorphosis will have begun at his neckjoint and it will go on till it has changed his likings first and then his reasoning, which will follow his likings as the feet of a hungry dog follow his nose. I'll have none of your clerkly gentility. I might end by collecting greasy pence from poor men to buy myself a fine coat and a glutton's dinner, on pretence of serving the poor men . . . I should like well enough to be another sort of demagogue if I could." Fortunately he only exercised his demagogical powers on a private audience.

If any character in this book is incredible it is Felix, who speaks a language as far from reality as anything in *Romola*. He is not the Warwickshire working-man, so well known to George Eliot, but a carefully excogitated urban working-man whose voice she could never have heard except in fantasy – no one ever heard such a voice in real life. As Leslie Stephen wrote: 'He represents the afterthought of the judicious sociologist and not the man of flesh and blood who was the object of the actual conditions.'

Stephen also attacks him for venting his opinions not on political opponents, but in unmanly hectoring of the unfortunate Esther. His rudeness to her is mixed with sadism ("I should like to come and scold her every day and make her cry and cut her fine hair off") and also with a sense of inferiority. Once she puts him in his place.

' "One sort of fine ladyism is as good as another," said Felix.

' "No, indeed. Pardon me," said Esther. "A real fine lady does not wear clothes that flare in people's eyes, or use importunate scents, or make a noise as she moves: she is something refined and graceful, and charming, and never obtrusive."

' "O yes," said Felix contemptuously. "And she reads Byron also, and admires Childe Harold – gentlemen of unspeakable woes, who employ a hairdresser, and look seriously at themselves in the glass."

'Esther reddened, and gave a little toss. Felix went on triumphantly. "A fine lady is a squirrel-headed thing, with small airs and motions, about as applicable to the business of life as a pair of tweezers to the clearing of a forest. Ask your father what those old persecuted emigrant Puritans would have done with fine-lady wives and daughters."

' "O there is no danger of such misalliances," said Esther. "Men who are unpleasant companions and make frights of themselves, are sure to get wives tasteless enough to suit them." '

Esther has won.[6]

Unhappily for Esther, Felix is of good appearance. They fall in love, and for Felix to love is to wish to improve.

' "You said you didn't mind about people having right opinions," said Felix, "so that they had good taste. Now I want you to see what shallow stuff that is" ' (ch. 10).

It is not such "shallow stuff" as it looks. There are good men in every camp, and their contradictory opinions cannot all be right: what makes them acceptable, even to their opponents, is something not unlike "good taste".

Felix abuses language much more than Esther does: "It comes to the same thing, thoughts, opinions, knowledge, are only a sensibility to facts and ideas. If I understand a geometrical problem, it is because I have a sensibility to the way in which lines and figures are related to each other: and I want you to see that the creature who has the sensibilities that you call taste, and not the sensibilities that you call opinions, is simply a lower, pettier sort of being."

---

[6] 'Notwithstanding the mighty effects of the Pilgrim Fathers' voyage, they and their standard of perfection are rightly judged when we figure to ourselves Shakespeare or Virgil—souls in which sweetness and light, and all that in human nature is most humane, were eminent—accompanying them on their voyage, and think what intolerable company Shakespeare and Virgil would have found them'; Matthew Arnold, *Culture and Anarchy*, ch. 1.

Esther yields too easily to his hectoring and his false argument, being sensitive to his personal attractions. Leslie Stephen thought that George Eliot (as in the case of Tom and Maggie) believed that women liked being treated like slaves; possibly she thought they liked being treated like spaniels – and perhaps we may throw the blame for this on Isaac.

Felix continues to lecture her even more unfairly. "I can't bear to see you going the way of the foolish women who spoil men's lives. Men can't help loving them, and so they make themselves slaves to the petty desires of petty creatures. That's the way those who might do better spend their lives for nought – get checked in every great effort – toil with brain and limb for things which have no more to do with a manly life than tarts and confectionery. That's what makes women a curse: all life is stunted to suit their littleness. That's why I'll never love, if I can help it; and if I love, I'll bear it and never marry."

In such a case, he might have spared her this lecture; he is apt to address her, and even himself, as if he were addressing a public meeting – not that he is any good at public speaking.

Esther surprises us by her lack of spirit.

"I am glad to see at least that you wear the liberal colours," says Harold.

' "I fear I must confess that it is more from love of blue than from love of liberalism. Yellow opinions could only have brunettes on their side." Esther spoke in her usual pretty fluency, but she had no sooner uttered these words than she thought how angry they would have made Felix' (ch. 16).

We are not told that she felt remorse, though it seems to be implied – and very tame-spirited that would be, all the more because she cared for Felix.

The chief interest in Felix as a radical is in the contrast between him and the other radical, Harold Transome. Harold's attitude is not unlike that of his uncle, Jack Lingon, rector of Little Treby: 'In these hopeless times nothing was left to men of sense and good family but to retard the national ruin by declaring themselves Radical, and take the inevitable process of changing everything out of the hands of beggarly demagogues and purse-proud tradesmen' (ch. 2). Felix was a man of the people.

He comes into contact with Harold's agent, John Johnson, at

the inn at Sproxton. "This is a crisis, and we must exert ourselves," says Johnson. "We've got Reform, gentlemen, but now the thing is to make Reform work. It's a crisis – I pledge you my word it's a crisis. . ." (ch. 11).

'Felix felt himself in danger of getting in a rage. There is hardly any mental misery, worse than that of having our own serious phrases, our own rooted beliefs, caricatured by a charlatan or a hireling.'

To Felix (as to George Eliot, deeply interested in the Reform Bill of 1867 – a year after the completion of the book) the important thing was the clean fighting of elections without bribery. Like her friend, Frederic Harrison, she thought extended franchise and the ballot were useless as long as bribery continued.

Felix discovers that Harold Transome's agent intended to bribe rough, voteless colliers and navvies of Sproxton with the chance of extra drunkenness, so that they might form a posse on his side at the nomination and polling.

"I'm a Radical myself," he says, "and mean to work all my life long against privilege, monopoly and oppression. But I would rather be a livery-servant proud of my master's title, than I would seem to make common cause with scoundrels who turn the best hopes of men into by-words for cant and dishonesty" (ch. 16).

Harold is personally innocent, though he has left the electioneering business uncritically to Jermyn, and thus to the latter's factotum, Johnson. His own intervention is too late to make much difference.

During the Treby Riot on election day – a fine crowd scene, inspired by George Eliot's recollection of a riot in Nuneaton – Felix rescues Sprott, the unpopular manager of a colliery, by tying him up. A constable, Tucker, misunderstands Felix's action, and assaults him. Felix throws the constable to the ground, thereby causing his death from spinal concussion.

Frederic Harrison was again consulted about legal procedure.

'The verdict must be for "Manslaughter" only,' he wrote. 'As I said you cannot mix up assault, riot, etc. in this indictment. I mentioned that the killing of a constable in the lawful execution of his duty is not Manslaughter but *Murder*. So far as I now remember the riot and scuffle Tucker was *un*lawfully

attacking Felix – not trying to arrest him in due course. This
would be Manslaughter, but the distinctions in such a case as
this would be fine.

'The "Sentence" which I thought wrong (it is now 2 years
only of imprisonment and was 3) is I find after some searching
right. How did you light on the vii Georg: IV which made
manslaughter 4 years imprisonment?'[7]

Harrison had already explained the course the trial must
take. '(a) Speech of prosecutor (b) witnesses against prisoner
(c) speech of prisoner (d) witnesses for prisoner, to character
last (e) reply of prosecutor . . . By permission of the judge and
at his examination, witnesses might be called at any moment *in
favorem vitae* . . . Thus if you need it Esther's speech *might* come
in anywhere (last or not) by special leave of the judge . . .
Prisoners might have the assistance of counsel even before
1835 to cross-examine witnesses, but *not to speak*. So that Felix
would be quite consistent in rejecting counsel's aid.'[8]

In the end Esther volunteered to give and gave her evidence
to character after all the other witnesses for the prisoner, and
immediately before the prosecutor's reply (ch. 46). Though her
speech contained no evidence, many people present were
greatly moved by its sincerity, and a meeting was held next
day at the White Hart at Loamford. Philip Debarry, absent in
London, had urged his father, Sir Maximus, and his uncle the
Rev. Augustus, to exert themselves for Felix. Nor was Harold
Transome backward. The object was to secure a pardon, but
the meeting was broken up by Jermyn. He forced his way
to Harold – who had refused to see him – and played his last
card, declaring: "*I am your father*" (ch. 47).

A pardon was obtained for Felix, and he was freed.

'This history is chiefly concerned with the private life of a few
men and women; but there is no private life which has not been
determined by a wider public life' (ch. 3). Yet the most vital
part of *Felix Holt* is not at all determined by public events. The
story of Mrs Transome and the lawyer Jermyn, and Harold
their son, could have been as far isolated from the social and
political life around them as any story by Jane Austen, Henry
James or Ivy Compton-Burnett – and it would have gained

[7] Haight *Letters*, iv, p. 264.   [8] ibid., p. 260.

much from the isolation in which these purer artists would have set it. All that the story requires is a mother, ruling an estate for a long absent son; her adultery in the past with a shady lawyer, who has profited by her secret to bleed the estate, and the return of their son, who is sure to look into matters.

Mrs Transome is the only interesting character in the novel, and her story is presented with such force that we may wholeheartedly agree with Dr Leavis that George Eliot shows herself as a great creative artist in this part of the book. Here is a heroine formed out of no self-indulgent fancies: George Eliot could not have wished to be like Mrs Transome. But this figure of creative reflection is intensely living, as living as Felix is lifeless.

As Arabella Lingon, member of a poor but excellent family, she had been glad enough to marry Mr Transome – miserable creature though he was – and to become (after Lady Debarry of Treby Manor) the second lady of the neighbourhood. By her husband she had a feckless, worthless son, baptized by the true family name, Durfey. The young lawyer, Matthew Jermyn, a vulgar, rising man, was the father of her second son, Harold. Leslie Stephen said that he would have liked to know more about this affair, but it is easy to imagine how it came about. On one side there was a handsome, dissatisfied woman, without principles to guide her, or sufficient intellectual interests to occupy her by no means contemptible mind; on the other side there was a full-blooded, ambitious man with whom she was thrown into close contact. There had at one time been some suspicions about her in the county (ch. 7) and the Debarrys had heard her talked of; and there is one extremely subtle hint (ch. 42) that Mr Transome had been used to finding his wife in Jermyn's company. Her maid – still called 'Denner' though now married to Hickes the butler – knows everything, and says nothing.

'As Mrs Transome descended the stone staircase in her old black velvet and point, her appearance justified Denner's personal compliment. She had that high-born imperious air that would have marked her as an object of hatred and reviling by a revolutionary mob. Her person was too typical of social distinctions to be passed by with indifference by anyone;

it would have fitted an empress in her own right, who had had to rule in spite of faction, to dare the violation of treaties, to grasp after new territories, to be defiant in desperate circumstances, and to feel a woman's hunger of heart for ever unsatisfied' (ch. 1). She is as splendid as Proust's Queen of Naples – the only character in George Eliot's novels great enough to be called tragic; and she is in the typical predicament of the tragic heroine in that she desires contradictory and irreconcilable things – her son's return and the safeguarding of her secret. Felix is never privileged to meet her, but he would probably be too insensitive and too firmly prejudiced to see in her the walking refutation of his stupid remarks about 'fine ladyism'.

Mrs Transome is as successful a creation as Felix is the reverse. No doubt George Eliot, who knew nothing of the urban artisan, had here rather more to go on. In her youth she had known women who were dominant in county society, and Charles Eliot Norton may have been exaggerating when he wrote in 1869: 'She is not received in general society, and the women who visit her are either so émancipée [sic] as not to mind what the world says about them, or have no social position to maintain. Lewes dines out a good deal, and some of the men with whom he dines go without their wives to his house on Sundays.'[9] However Lord Acton suggested that about 1867 'the hard barrier yielded to her prodigious fame',[10] and even by the time she was writing *Felix Holt* she was no longer such a pariah.

Mrs Transome's life has not been poisoned by her secret – 'her part in life had been that of the clever sinner' (ch. 1) – so much as by 'a hungry desire that her first, ricketty, ugly, imbecile child should die, and leave room for her darling, of whom she could be proud'. For George Eliot it always seems exaggeratedly wicked to desire someone's death (or merely the consequences of it) – thus Godfrey Cass is severely rebuked for hoping that his detested wife will be found dead – and yet death is not necessarily an evil, and might be the best thing for Molly and for Durfey. George Eliot can never (quite) bring her characters to kill. Hetty (we feel) has been wrongly convicted of infanti-

[9] cit. Haight *Letters*, VI, p.7.
[10] Haight *Biography*, p. 393.

cide; and there is no case for a jury against Bulstrode or Gwendolen Harleth. Neither Godfrey Cass nor Mrs Transome did anything to implement their uncharitable wishes.

Meanwhile Mrs Transome had to do her duty in managing a ravaged estate, though not daring to hinder the further ravages made upon it by her former lover, the lawyer. Then Durfey died, and Harold returned as a rich businessman from Smyrna; and Mrs Transome had to face the situation.

'Mrs Transome knew in her inmost soul that those relations which had sealed her lips on Jermyn's conduct in business matters, had been with him a ground for presuming that he should have impunity in any lax dealing into which circumstances had led him. She knew that she herself had endured all the more privations because of his dishonest selfishness. And how Harold's long-deferred heirship, and his return with unexpected penetration, activity and assertion of mastery, had placed them both in the full presence of a difficulty which had been prepared by the years of vague uncertainty over issues.'

The looked-forward-to moment of her triumph, the return of Harold as heir, is the beginning of the long process by which her sin is to find her out. It is very soon clear to her that her son will be pitiless about the malversation of his property; it is equally clear that Jermyn will stick at nothing to defend himself.

' "Bear anything from him rather than quarrel with him."

' "A man cannot make a vow not to quarrel," said Jermyn, who was already a little irritated by the implication that Harold might be disposed to use him roughly. "A man's temper may get the better of him at any moment. I am not prepared to bear *anything*."

' "Good God!" said Mrs Transome, taking her hand from his arm, "is it possible you don't feel how horrible it would be!" ' (ch. 9).

He does not; he has forgotten their old affair except insofar as he can use it for a bargaining point. Mrs Transome remembers, and cannot forgive herself for her connexion with this coarse, underbred swindler; and she knows how Harold will loathe him for a father.

Finally Jermyn, having been struck across the face by Harold with a whip, comes out with his story – and in the looking-glass Harold sees 'the hated fatherhood reasserted' (ch. 47).

The hero of the occasion is Sir Maximus Debarry, a fine gentleman of the old school.

'Harold felt himself supported by the arm. It was Sir Maximus Debarry who had taken hold of him.

' "Leave the room, sir!" the baronet said to Jermyn, in a voice of imperious scorn. "This is a meeting of gentlemen."

' "Come, Harold," he said, in the old friendly voice, "come away with me." '

'Harold Transome was a clever, frank, good-natured egoist, not stringently consistent, but without any disposition to falsity; proud, but with a pride that was moulded in an individual rather than an hereditary form; unspeculative, unsentimental, unsympathetic; fond of sensual pleasures, but disinclined to all vice, and attached as a healthy, clear-sighted person, to all conventional morality, construed with a certain freedom, like doctrinal articles to which public order may require subscription' (ch. 8). A pleasant practical unidealistic *homme moyen sensuel*, fond of his comforts, but anxious for the comfort of those around him, if incapable or unwilling to enter deeply into their feelings.

It was through no fault of his that his election agents behaved so badly: 'He had tried to hinder them, and had tried in vain' (ch. 34). He resolved to do all he could to save Felix (ch. 35). Nor was his conduct other than honourable when Esther's claim came up. He is hard to his mother at the moment of revelation – but he has cause to be overcome with disgust at the idea that Jermyn is his father.

To Esther he is uniformly kind and chivalrous: it is even with exaggerated scrupulosity that he withdraws his suit for her hand, after learning of his parentage. "I shut myself out from the chance of trying, after today, to induce you to accept anything which others may regard as speckled and stained by any obloquy, however slight" (ch. 49). He is still the legal son of Mr Transome, and it is certain that the county will follow the example of Sir Maximus and rally round him as Transome of Transome Court. He is quite a good enough match for Esther Lyon, if she liked him – and a natural son of Mrs

Transome is a far better match than 'honest madam's issue',
if the 'honest madam' be Mrs Holt. Moreover Harold offers
her a mission, more convincing than any Felix has to offer.
The one moment when this worthy and uninteresting young
woman comes to life – apart from the trial scene – is when she
comforts Mrs Transome. "If that dear thing will marry you,
Harold," says the latter to her son, "it will make up to you for
a great deal" (ch. 51).

Esther, however, is in love with Felix. One critic complains
that, as the author has written her book, this is no more than a
'personal preference':[11] but one may wonder what but
'personal preference' ought to influence choice in marriage,
and if any normal young woman has ever preferred one suitor to
another because of the greater purity of his political principles.
She gave up the claim to the Transome estates, but was
practical enough to retain a small allowance, and annuities for
her father and for Felix's mother. 'Why,' asks the same critic,[12]
'it should be better to accept Esther's money than his father's
is not revealed.' It needs no revelation. Felix had no objection
to money in itself, but the Holt money came from the sale of
harmful medicines, and we know of no dishonourable source
for the Transome allowances.

It is tempting to compare this novel with one far greater,
with Dickens's *Bleak House*, though I do not know that any
influence has ever been suggested. Here again we have a lady
in a prominent position, guilty of an illicit love affair in time
past, and mother of a natural child. Lady Dedlock too waits,
and generally in her country house, for the revelation that is
going to ruin her. Here again the family lawyer is the agent of
destruction. A pleasant young woman – again called Esther –
is the good angel. Esther Summerson (like Esther Lyon) connects
the theme of the unfortunate lady with the other themes of the
book – and these themes are connected with wider social
interests, and the law.

At the end Esther Lyon settles down to a cosy married life
with Felix: he aspires to set up a library for working men, and
no doubt he does so. He has, apparently, come down without
much ado from the 'higher' to the 'lower' rule, and Esther will

[11] *Critical Essays*, p. 110.   [12] ibid., p. 108.

not obviously be invited to a life of greater usefulness than that
which she might have passed on 'cushions' at Transome Court.
The Holt couple may be compared with Esther Summerson
and her husband, who settle down to a quiet life of more
evident usefulness – though they had never aimed at anything
higher.

Lady Dedlock is far less interesting than Mrs Transome.
Dickens at this time knew nothing of the London society in
which she played a leading role, whereas George Eliot was
fully competent to imagine the Loamshire background of Mrs
Transome. But the symbolic background to Honoria Dedlock's
suffering – the rain in Lincolnshire – raises her story to a
tragic level. We do not care to remember the Dantesque
'fallen leaves' (ch. 9) of Transome Court.

Jermyn's relationship with Mrs Transome is entirely
comprehensible, while Tulkinghorn's machinations against
Lady Dedlock are motiveless and incredible: moreover a great
number of coincidences, some impossible, come to his help.
'Poor untidy life' (said Gissing) 'disclaims all question on these
doings.' We are asked to believe that Lady Dedlock's lover,
when he disappeared over the side of a ship, took all her letters
with him (presumably in a water-proof bag); that Lady
Dedlock, who supposed him dead, should years later recognise
his calligraphy, though under the disguise of a 'law hand';
that the death of his landlord, by 'spontaneous combustion',
should make her wrongly suppose that her letters had been
burned – and that is not all. George Eliot's only piece of
artificial plot manipulation is the opium sleep of Christian,
and the improbability of his carrying Bycliffe's relics about
with him.

Nevertheless Dickens's Esther – and the coincidence of the
name surely proves that there was no conscious influence –
connects the theme of the sinful lady with an equally interesting
theme, the moral collapse of Richard Carstone, the victim of
his 'expectations' in a Chancery case. And here we have
Dickens treating the law imaginatively and symbolically.
We know none of the legal details in *Jarndyce and Jarndyce*, but
we are profoundly interested in it; on the other hand we care
nothing about *Bycliffe versus Transome*, about which we know as
much as is to be known by the layman. The only victim in the

latter case was Esther's father, whom we have never met. Nor could any possible result much concern us; we do not want Esther to have the property (nor does she), but if it came to the point Harold could probably afford to buy her out.

Above all, in *Bleak House*, we are continually aware of the 'bleak house' of England in 1851: the political deadlock is treated frivolously enough, with its Coodles and Doodles, but while it continues there is little hope of clearing up the slums, like Tom-all-alone's, or of dispersing the fog of Chancery: and it is their effluvia that is experienced throughout the book. In the early chapter of *Felix Holt* there is at least an equal grasp of the problems of England in 1833: George Eliot had been at great trouble to read up the period, and she had a mind far more capable of seeing things steadily than that of Dickens. Nevertheless, the unreality of Felix himself deadens those parts of the book where he is predominant. George Eliot had not Dickens's imaginative power of rendering law and politics symbolically; she was too little of a poet. Nor had she Trollope's gift of interesting herself creatively in them. We can only wish that she had rejected one of her two initial themes, and had found some other way of making Jermyn fall into his own trap – any other way would have been less complicated. Critics have well pointed out that the Transome tragedy could have as well been acted to its end if Harold had stood successfully in the conservative interest (or better, not at all) and had there been no missing heir to the estates.

The book as a whole is a failure, though it contains the strongest work that George Eliot had done up to date. It is amazing to think that contemporary readers knew whole passages by heart, and recited them as if they were saying quatrains out of *In Memoriam*. We must be deeply grateful to those readers who so greatly overrated this prentice work of George Eliot's later period, and to George Henry Lewes, who kept disparaging reviews from her. There can seldom have been such an occasion for a reviewer to prick the bubble of an inflated reputation as after *Romola* and *Felix Holt*. Yet had this been done – for we know her morbid sensitiveness – the author would not have given us her masterpiece, *Middlemarch*, towards which we can feel she was groaning and travailing here.

VII   Middlemarch

Middlemarch is George Eliot's masterpiece, the one book in which she consistently and indubitably shows herself a great author, and which deserves European recognition: it is the finest fruit of her mature talent.

Dr Leavis was therefore right to attack that assessment of her work that used to be popular – that is, the judgment that she never properly got her second wind, and that when she had come to the end of her Warwickshire recollections there was nothing but laborious brain-work left to her: that the novelist died after *Silas Marner*, and only the massive, uncreative moralist was left.

He complained that 'the appreciation of George Eliot's *oeuvre* has not been put on a critical basis and reduced to consistency'. This omission he tried to correct, but perhaps he sought too firm a critical basis and too rigid a consistency. He attempted to achieve this by some devaluation of the earlier work (a little excessive in the case of *Adam Bede*); and by some over-praise of *Felix Holt*, which precedes *Middlemarch*, and of *Daniel Deronda*, which follows it.

In *Felix Holt* and in *Daniel Deronda* there are certainly very fine things, passages superior to anything in the early books, and on a level with the great themes of *Middlemarch*. On the other hand, the bad things in these books are infinitely tedious and very much worse than anything she had done since the Clerical Scenes. Dr Leavis frankly admits that only the Transome story is worth having in *Felix Holt*, and speaks of the 'wordy impotence' of a great part of *Daniel Deronda*.

Many will prefer achievement on a smaller scale, but still a notable achievement, in *Adam Bede* and *Silas Marner* to the failure on a grander scale in the later books. Moreover there is no need for 'consistency' in the appraisement of George Eliot's work. There is no reason to say, as a general statement, that it improved or deteriorated after *Romola*. Each book is a thing in itself.

If we must have a formula, it might be said that George Eliot was in *Felix Holt* starting out, with far greater powers, on her second apprenticeship, and that she reached her second maturity in *Middlemarch*.

This novel, with all its connecting themes, gives a whole picture of provincial life. It would take many volumes of Balzac's *Comédie humaine* to cover so many sides of life, so many different pursuits – and there are parts of the book that required powers even superior to his. It is particularly remarkable that a woman novelist, whose life had been for years rather secluded, should venture to write about the working lives of so many people. E. M. Forster has observed of the difference between Man in Life and Man in Fiction, that *homo fictus* has very little work to do, and spends an altogether disproportionate amount of time on love. Work is, on the whole, more important to people in Middlemarch – even emotionally – than their relations with one another. Most of the characters earn their living, and we see them doing so. Those who are not under that necessity have nearly always some serious occupations that keep them busy.

The lives that George Eliot thoroughly knows and understands and completely portrays are those of good or bad landowners (Brooke and Chettam), of small town business men (Bulstrode and Vincy), of different types of clergy (Farebrother and Tyke), of a builder and land-agent (Caleb Garth), and of poor Fred Vincy and his amateur horse-coping. Her 'laborious brainwork', which was also intensely creative, enabled her to render the lives of Casaubon and Lydgate. A great deal of what she knew of people's daily lives, and of the whole network that is Middlemarch, she had learned in Warwickshire. This time she did not attempt such a figure as Felix Holt, about whom neither instinct nor experience had anything to teach her.

'There is no private life which has not been determined by a wider public life,' wrote George Eliot in *Felix Holt* – where she failed to illustrate this point, for many of the strands do not come together. In *Middlemarch* everyone is firmly set in his place in provincial society. George Eliot has even overdone 'the stealthy convergence of human lots', and the 'slow preparation of effects from one life on another', for eighteen of the principal characters – that is, everyone of importance except Fare-brother – are connected by a continuous relationship by blood or marriage.[1] It was well enough, early in the book, to make Featherstone uncle by one marriage to Mary Garth, and by another to Fred and Rosamond Vincy. This is only a compli-cation of the connection between Hetty and Dinah in *Adam Bede*. But it is a shock (and an improbability) to find Bulstrode revealed as the step-grandfather of Will Ladislaw.

Each of the main characters is very much more than a character; he is an embodiment of an important theme in the book.

Edward Casaubon's name 'carried an impressiveness hardly to be measured without a precise chronology of scholarship' (ch. 1). We may not quite know what this clumsy sentence means, but the suggestion is that it is a learned name. This is true: it was the name of two eminent scholars, Isaac and Meric Casaubon, the first of whom was the subject of a book published by Mark Pattison, rector of Lincoln College, Oxford, in 1875.[2] The studies of Pattison were well known before the publication of the book, and it is unthinkable that George Eliot gave the name by accident. Pattison's academic ideal was research – in opposition to the more liberal and literary aims of Benjamin Jowett, the Master of Balliol, and translator of Plato. George Eliot knew Pattison, and was devoted to his wife Emilia, whom she often addresses as "my pretty" or as *figliuolina*. A novelist is not a biographer, and there is no need for his portrait of an original to be truthful – indeed there will be good reasons against making it too obviously recognisable. Pattison (author of a very unlikeable autobiography) had faults and virtues that Casaubon lacked; in particular he was a much more eminent and successful scholar.

[1] See pp. 60–1.

[2] It is, however, likely that the name 'Casibon' was known to George Eliot before she wrote the Clerical Scenes. It occurs in a pamphlet entitled 'A True Relation of the Apparition of one Mrs VEAL The Next Day after Her Death; to one Mrs BARGRAVE at *Canterbury*. The 8th of *September*, 1705.' This is a probable source for a scene in 'Janet's Repentance'. (I owe this reference to my former pupil, Mr Ion Zottos.)

Conjectures about other sources for the character of Casaubon[3] are interesting, and probably contain truth. George Eliot had composed an imaginary proposal of marriage by a 'Professor Bücherwurm' in 1846; her friend Herbert Spencer and her former lover Brabant may have provided traits – and Eliza Lynn Linton believed the latter to be the original. An eighteenth-century work by Jacob Bryant, *A New System: or An Analysis of Ancient Mythology*, may have in part inspired Casaubon's *Key*; and something may have been derived from *The Progress of the Intellect as Exemplified in the Religious Development of the Greeks and Hebrews*, a book by Robert William Mackay published by another lover, John Chapman, in 1850 and reviewed by George Eliot.

Nevertheless, the unpublished autobiography of Sir Charles Dilke, the second husband of Emilia Pattison, is decisive.

'I had on the appearance of *Middlemarch* been one of those who saw how George Eliot had drawn from Emilia Strong [Mrs Pattison's maiden name] the opinions of Dorothea Brooke and how she tried to draw a view of the Reverend Mark Pattison's character in that of the Reverend Mr Casaubon – to whom she indeed gave a name which could only show that she meant Pattison and meant to be known to mean him. The portrait of the author of the life of Casaubon, under the name of Casaubon, was a cruel one. George Eliot evidently, though she professed friendship for Pattison, had a personal dislike and contempt for the man and tried to show it. Her portrait differs from the original in the point of total disregard for the real learning which Pattison undoubtedly possessed . . . George Eliot must have worked hard through all her Oxford friends and through Pattison himself (for she knew him at one time very well, and he was a very intimate friend at one moment of George Henry Lewes) to get at every fact which had a bearing on his character. For example Casaubon's letter to Dorothea at the beginning of the 5th chapter of *Middlemarch*, from what George Eliot herself told me in 1875, must have been very

---

[3] Richard Ellman, in the *Times Literary Supplement*, 16 February, 1973.

near the letter that Pattison actually wrote, and the reply very much the same.'[4]

It is impossible to say, and probably George Eliot could not have said, where her idea of Casaubon began, and it is most unlikely that all the contributory sources have yet been named. Proust said of 'keys' to his novel: 'There are so many to each door, that in fact there is none.' And: 'There is no name of a fictitious character under which the writer could not put sixty names of people seen.'[5] But one of the names for Casaubon is certainly Pattison, and it seems equally certain that in this character the author was working off a personal spite.

The appearance of friendship with the Pattisons was maintained. However, when Rhoda Broughton drew the rector as Professor Forth in *Belinda* (a character whose main trait was miserliness) Pattison called on her one day, and had himself announced by the name she had given him. He is not recorded to have announced himself at the Priory as 'Mr Casaubon' – too much fat would then have been in the fire.[6] But Emilia Pattison told her friend Ellen Smith that she would never read *Middlemarch*.[7]

Rhoda Broughton gave Forth Pattison's beard, George Eliot made Casaubon 'remarkably like the portrait of Locke' (ch. 2). This was wise, for even if we do not exactly remember what Locke looked like, the name at once carries with it a notion of philosophical profundity and a sense of the past. If, however, he really resembled Locke, Casaubon would not have served

[4] BM. Add. MS. 49392 ff. 138–45, cit. John Sparrow in the *Times Literary Supplement*, 16 March 1973. Mr Sparrow (rather charitably) suggests in *Mark Pattison and the Idea of a University* (Cambridge 1967), pp. 16–17, that George Eliot was deliberately avenging Emilia: 'strong action by one high-minded woman on behalf of another.'

[5] cit. Liddell, *Treatise*, p. 102.

[6] And the Sibyl was used to kid glove treatment. More liberties might be taken with 'our dauntless, our relentless, our impossible Rhoda' (as Henry James called her), whose social position was unimpaired, and who had a sense of humour in private life.

[7] Though it is certain that she did so: *see* John Sparrow, l.c., p. 16. In parenthesis I may mention my own first novel, *The Almond Tree* (1938), which was inspired by the Pattison papers in the Bodleian, to which I had access. I altered the date and the setting, but endeavoured to make my 'Dr Ramus' a really learned man.

Naumann well as a model for St Thomas Aquinas, who was inordinately fat.

Casaubon's speech had a 'balanced sing-song neatness'. He must be over fifty (though we are told he is about forty-seven, twenty-seven years older than Dorothea) because he has been studying for his *Key to all Mythologies* for more than twenty-five years. He would hardly have begun this before taking his degree.

He is 'squarson' of Lowick, near Middlemarch. He had entered the Church and was rector of the parish when his elder brother's death made him also lord of the manor. In the world of Middlemarch Casaubon therefore stands comparison with other landlords and clergymen, and he stands the comparison well. By his learning he reflects credit both on the Church and the squirearchy; nor are his duties as parish priest and landowner neglected. They are largely deputed to his curate, Tucker, who serves the church, and is able to assure Dorothea (ch. 9) that everyone is well off in the village. Casaubon does not take the personal interest that is taken by Sir James Chettam of Freshitt Hall, but the result seems to be as good; and he is an infinitely better landlord than Brooke of Tipton Grange. It goes without saying that he is an infinitely better scholar than Brooke, who is a mere amateur, who has 'been into' everything in his life, but never deeply, and remembers nothing. He serves, even, as a caricature of Casaubon.

A radical demagogue called Casaubon 'the learned straw-chopping incumbent', and Cadwallader the 'angling incumbent'; he might have added that Farebrother was the 'whist-playing incumbent'. All these types of clergy have their place in the Anglican tradition, and Casaubon's is surely the most honourable.

He is to stand or fall by his work, the *Key to all Mytho-logies*. What he is aiming at is a kind of *Praeparatio Evangelica*, designed to show that myths are corruptions of a tradition originally revealed (ch. 3). When we are first told about it, he lets Dorothea know that it is something that 'had been attempted before, but not with that thoroughness, justice of comparison and effectiveness' at which he aimed. It even appeared that he had a comprehensive view of his subject (if we are thus to interpret a very clumsy sentence beginning with an unattached participle): 'Having once mastered the true position and taken a firm footing there, the vast field of mythical constructions became intelligible, nay, luminous with the reflected light of correspondences.' Dorothea was 'altogether captivated by the wide embrace of this conception'.

That is how she starts off – but when there is a danger that Casaubon will die, and leave her with his work to finish, she sees that she may have to spend years in 'sorting out what might be called shattered mummies and fragments of a tradition which was itself a mosaic, wrought from crushed ruins – sorting them for a theory already withered in the birth like an elfin child' (ch. 48). This looks as if Casaubon had himself given birth to (or miscarried of) a theory, and not at all as if he were trying to do better what had been already done – still less as if 'the vast field of mythical constructions' had been 'intelligible' and 'luminous' to him.

It may be doubted if George Eliot had really made up her mind as to what Casaubon was about; she intended him to be a scholar, to give his life to his work, to have grave misgivings about it, and to be a failure. The personal and private life that results is, of course, beautifully worked out, but it does not seem as if the author deserves all the praise she is given for her skill in depicting the professional life of a scholar.

She might perhaps be defended by an obstinate supporter against the inconsistency of the two passages. It might be said that the latter represents the view that Dorothea had come to adopt, while the former had been her first glowing (and quite false) notion of Casaubon's plan. This will not really do – the first passage makes assertions that cannot so easily be brushed aside. Moreover it appears that George Eliot is confused about the details of the *Key to all Mythologies* as she was about the sum.

A characteristic of Casaubon's mode of work is that he fills an infinity of note-books in his 'laborious uncreative hours' (ch. 10), and fears to write them up into any kind of work that can be given to the public – unless it be some short pamphlet or *parergon* (ch. 29) of a highly specialised nature. 'Poor Mr Casaubon himself was lost among small closets and winding stairs, and in an agitated dimness about the Cabeiri, or in an exposure of other mythologists' ill-considered parallels, easily lost sight of any purpose which had prompted him to these labours. With his taper stuck before him he forgot the absence of windows, and in bitter manuscript notations about the solar deities, he had become indifferent to the sunlight' (ch. 20).

This sounds as if he were the sort of grubbing scholar who cannot see the wood for the trees. Will Ladislaw is a person of a very superficial mind – but he may not be entirely mistaken in saying that Casaubon is badly handicapped in this sort of study because he is unable to consult the work of German scholars (ch. 21), particularly orientalists (ch. 22). Nevertheless the handicap might not be so very great in 1831, when Latin was still the international language of scholarship.

Work such as this is minutely exact and extremely vulnerable to criticism. And yet Dorothea is later made to reflect on its unreality. 'Mr Casaubon's theory of the elements which made the seed of all tradition was not likely to bruise itself unaware against discoveries . . . it was as free from interruption as a plan for threading the stars together.' She goes on to think of it as 'questionable riddle-guessing' (ch. 48). It sounds as if it were like one of those bedlamitical theories about the authorship of Shakespeare's plays invented in the last century by American matrons who had nothing better to do. Such theories are, strictly speaking, irrefutable, for they afford no purchase for reason; and a marked thing that their inventors have in common is a fanatical faith in their nonsense. Casaubon's is a very different psychology, and his *parerga* are very likely to be bruised when they are 'scanned by Brasenose' (ch. 29).

It cannot be said, on the strength of Casaubon, that George Eliot completely understands the scholar's life – but what she does know all about (and admirably uses to give this character greater authenticity) is the life of the writer. 'There are some kinds of authorship in which by far the largest result is the uneasy susceptibility accumulated in the consciousness of the author' (ch. 42). Casaubon had: 'a morbid consciousness that others did not give him the place which he had not demonstrably merited – a perpetual suspicious conjecture that the views entertained of him were not to his advantage – a melancholy absence of passion in his efforts at achievement, and a passionate resistance to the confession that he had achieved nothing.' George Eliot could have said: 'I am Casaubon', as Flaubert said: 'Madame Bovary, c'est moi!'

Casaubon's 'blankness of sensibility' (ch. 10) when he is about to marry Dorothea is linked with the 'despair which sometimes threatened him while toiling in the morass of authorship without seeming nearer to the goal.' His soul was 'sensitive without being enthusiastic' (ch. 29), with a 'proud, narrow sensitiveness' that quivered 'threadlike in small currents of preoccupation'. Earlier, on his engagement to Dorothea, 'he determined to abandon himself to the stream of feeling, and perhaps was surprised to find what an exceedingly shallow rill it was' (ch. 7). A possible explanation of him might have been that he had simply left marriage and authorship too late, but George Eliot does not make this apology for him. He appears to have wished to leave behind him both children of his own, and a published book (ch. 29). Some readers have supposed that he was impotent – but had that been the case George Eliot would no doubt have made it clear. The implication is that he was sterile.[8]

Dorothea too quickly became his public. She was 'not only his wife: she was a personification of that shallow world which surrounds the ill-appreciated or desponding author' (ch. 20). Even on their wedding journey she had said: "I never heard you speak of the writing that is to be published." He came to fear her as a spy. Only too soon Ladislaw upset her by telling her that her husband could not get far without knowledge of German (ch. 21).

Like his house at Lowick, Casaubon is 'small-windowed' (ch. 9); he is odiously without first-hand taste or opinions.

' "Should you like to go to the Farnesina, Dorothea? It contains celebrated frescoes designed or painted by Raphael which most persons think it worth while to visit."

' "But do you care about them?" was always Dorothea's question.

' "They are, I believe, highly esteemed. Some of them represent the fable of Cupid and Psyche, which is probably

[8] Dorothea might have preferred Casaubon to be impotent; Emilia much disliked physical relations with Mark Pattison (Sparrow, l.c., p. 45).

the romantic invention of a literary period, and cannot, I
think, be reckoned as a genuine mythical product. But if you
like these wall-paintings we can easily drive thither; and you
will then, I think, have seen the chief works of Raphael, any of
which it were a pity to omit in a visit to Rome. He is the
painter who has been held to combine the most complete grace
of form with sublimity of expression. Such at least I have
gathered to be the opinion of conoscenti" ' (ch. 20).

Like his house, he constitutes a prison where Dorothea will
be buried alive (ch. 22). Ironically, she had wished to escape
from a social life 'which seemed nothing but a labyrinth of
petty courses, a walled up maze of small paths that led no
whither' (ch. 3). She had been attracted by seeing in Casaubon's
mind 'in labyrinthine extension every quality she herself
brought', and by the 'labyrinthine extent' of his projected
work. But she was to find him 'lost among small closets and
winding stairs' (ch. 20); he 'carried his taper among the
tombs of the past' (ch. 22). Dorothea's maid, Tantripp, was
sensitive to this atmosphere, and wished every book in the
library were built "into a caticom" for Casaubon (ch. 48).
Much the same metaphor is employed when we are told how
Casaubon envisaged Dorothea's widowhood: 'He willingly
imagined her toiling under the fetters of a promise to erect a
tomb with his name upon it' (ch. 50).

He had once been a real person, and had traces of it left:
'He was as genuine a character as any ruminant animal, and
he had not actively assisted in creating illusions about himself'
(ch. 30). On one occasion at least he showed real delicacy in
protecting Dorothea from a tiresome argument (ch. 2). We
know of his great generosity to Ladislaw's family (ch. 8), and
that in youth he had been human enough to have spiritual
conflicts (ch. 3). He could still be tender and considerate:
"Come, my dear, come. You are young, and need not to
extend your life by watching" (ch. 42). His jealousy of Ladislaw,
shown posthumously in his will, is at least a human trait –
unattractive though it is – and in character.[9]

At the last he has a spurt of energy that almost looks as if it

_____

[9] 'Il y a des cœurs delicats; quand cela se trouve avec un esprit sec,
celà fait des progrès merveilleux dans le pays de la jalousie', Mme de
Sévigné, II, p. 809 (Pléiade).

would achieve something. Dorothea is amazed at the 'birdlike speed with which his mind was surveying the ground where it had been creeping for years' (ch. 48). His principle of selection was 'to give adequate and not disproportionate illustration to each of the theses enumerated' in his introduction – and 'the second excursus on Crete' and other things came out. He was preparing the material for use by Dorothea after his death – and though one is thankful that she escaped promising its continuation, one is less certain that it would have been a hopeless task. The common estimate of it as 'preposterous'[10] is an exaggeration.

Lydgate, like Casaubon, has been very well understood in the pattern of his life, and in its distortion by circumstances. 'Only those who know the supremacy of the intellectual life – the life that has a seed of ennobling thought and purpose within it – can understand the grief of one who falls from that serene activity into the absorbing soul-wasting struggle with worldly annoyances' (ch. 73). He had quickly got deep into debt, and like others in that position 'was forced to think chiefly of release, though he had a scheme for the universe in his soul' (ch. 58). George Eliot knew well what the intellectual life demanded, and what it was like to be short of money, but one is not convinced that she knew very much about Lydgate's studies. It is true that she was writing about medical science as it was in 1831, but her touch is uncertain. One is not sure whether Lydgate means to make a name for himself in anatomy – his first love – and surgery, or in pathology (chh. 15–16). The mention of Bichat, Laennec, Louis, Raspail and Vesalius looks rather like name-dropping. George Eliot read up the subject, as she had read up so much for *Romola* – she might have developed the theme much better without it.

'His ardour was absorbed in love of his work and in the ambition of making his life recognised as a factor in the better life of mankind – like other heroes of science who had nothing but an obscure country practice to begin with' (ch. 16). This is convincing – and when we see him actually attending patients – Trumbull and Raffles in particular – he appears as a skilful and devoted practitioner. His great moment of excitement is disappointing: 'Lydgate felt a triumphant delight in his

---

[10] Haight *Biography*, p. 564.

studies and something like pity for those less lucky men who were not of his profession.' But this occurred after reading a book, not after original research.

Nevertheless, he is presented as an intelligent, enthusiastic young man, with a passion for his subject that Casaubon singularly lacks, and some twenty-five more years in which to achieve something. Also (most convincingly) he is hampered by difficulties that Casaubon knew nothing of, for he has financial independence and a docile wife. Moreover Casaubon is unaffected by anything that goes on at Middlemarch – he is, with Will Ladislaw, the only character who looks outside it for judgment; in his case to Oxford.

Farebrother warned Lydgate of the difficulty of steering his course: "Either you slip out of service altogether, and become good for nothing, or you wear the harness and draw a good deal where your yoke-fellows pull you" (ch. 17).

Soon Lydgate was 'feeling the hampering threadlike pressure of small social conditions, and their frustrating complexity' (ch. 18). It is this pressure that forces him (ironically) to vote – and with the publicity of the casting vote – against Farebrother and in favour of Tyke, Bulstrode's candidate for the hospital chaplaincy. He was inclined to support Farebrother (his friend), but also inclined in favour of Bulstrode (his patron). It could not be said that he would do *wrong* to support either, and it was his hope to avoid being involved in the election. An insulting word from a rival physician, Wrench, implying that he must follow Bulstrode, made him do so out of defiance.

The same pressure of Middlemarch is felt behind the scene in which Lydgate becomes engaged to Rosamond. 'The town's talk' (ch. 31) reports her as already engaged to him, because of his light attentions to her, and her rejection of another suitor. Her aunt, Harriet Bulstrode, brings the gossip to her; she also drops a hint to him, and he makes an effort to escape. Then he has an errand to her father (about his patient, Featherstone), and almost out of bravado risks going to the house instead of to the warehouse for 'momentary speculations as to all the possible grounds for Mrs Bulstrode's hints had managed to get woven like slight clinging hairs into the more substantial web of his thoughts'. He found Rosamond engaged in chain-work: she wept, and he was caught in the chain.

We are told that his weakness was that he was one of those 'whose distinguished mind is a little spotted with commonness' (ch. 15). The last word is used in a sense that is George Eliot's own. She does not mean that he was in any way vulgar or plebeian; after Sir James Chettam he is probably the most nearly patrician person in or near Middlemarch. She seems to mean 'ordinariness' – perhaps the presence of average or sub-average weakness in a mind so very much above the average. He has a degree of egoism and, though no slave to appearances, expects always to present an appearance appropriate to his station. He has never yet known what it was to want money, though he has hardly any of his own – the dangerous financial education of a cadet of good family. He has a lowish opinion of women – partly due to his rather improbable love for the French actress Laure, which preceded the action of the book. He means one day to marry a 'docile' wife (ch. 16).

Rosamond is his destruction. It is hard for us to believe completely in her power because, between the covers of a book, she loses all the advantage of her beauty – we can only hear of it, and of its effect on all beholders; but, unmoved by it, we want to wring that 'fair long neck' (ch. 31).

Lydgate, on the one hand, is a parallel and contrast to Casaubon – a different kind of failure in the intellectual life. On the other hand, in his feeling of vocation, he is an offset to Dorothea.

The rest of his story is interwoven with Rosamond's. She was the daughter of the mayor, Vincy, and belonged to the solid commercial society of Middlemarch; her mother (an inn-keeper's daughter) came from a slightly lower stratum, and she herself had been educated a little above her station at Mrs Lemon's academy. Alas, Mrs Lemon's academy only taught 'all that was demanded in the accomplished female – even to extras, such as the getting in and out of a carriage' (ch. 11), and her tiny mind was left satisfied with the silly poetesses of the 'Keepsake' (ch. 27). Her one gift was music, and her music was very remarkable and misleading. She was an admirable executant (ch. 16) and faithfully reproduced the manner of her music-master, who was a real musician. This is another proof of her actress-like temperament.

She may be compared and contrasted with her brother

Fred, an amiable youth, who certainly was less good a musician, and whose studies at Oxford had not gone at all deep. He had kept 'good company' and had learned habits of laziness and self-indulgence, no doubt; but he had been turned into a gentleman by his education, while Rosamond had only learned a little provincial refinement from Mrs Lemon. He had remained good-hearted, simple and unpretentious, with no desire to rise in society by entering the Church. He had a great contempt for the 'finicking notions' that Rosamond had acquired at school.

His old uncle-by-marriage, Featherstone, had indulged him, and his parents had taught him to expect to be the old man's heir. If he had been, he would have made a better owner of Stone Court than Rigg or Bulstrode. In the end he was established there as Mrs Bulstrode's bailiff, and he made a very good job of it.

Rosamond was less pliable. A 'terrible tenacity' (ch. 58) is her distinguishing characteristic. She has fallen in love with Lydgate because she sees him as a means to her own social advancement: she really did for a time *love* him for that. She valued his birth, and expected 'more social effects when his talent should have advanced him; but for her his professional and scientific ambition had no other relation to these desirable effects than if they had been the fortunate discovery of an ill-smelling oil.' Lydgate even wondered if she would kill him if he bored her, as Laure killed her husband. "It is the way with all women", he thought – until he remembered Dorothea, in misery about the interruption of Casaubon's labours: "He minds about nothing else – and I mind about nothing else."

Rosamond 'was by nature an actress of parts that entered into her physique: she even acted her own character, and so well, that she did not know it to be precisely her own' (ch. 12). With this actress temperament, and love of appearances, she had nothing to sustain her when she was alone. Though she was virtuous, she was ready to flirt with Ladislaw in order to flatter herself that he was in her power. When she first learned the strength of his feeling for Dorothea, 'she was oppressed by ennui, and by that dissatisfaction which in women's minds is continually turning into a trivial jealousy, referring to no real claims, springing from no deeper passion than the vague exactingness of egoism, and yet capable of impelling action as well as speech' (ch. 69). Her 'utter *ennui*' was further emphasised by the loss of her baby: she had miscarried, entirely through her own fault, because she had gone out riding in defiance of her husband's orders.

Lydgate has to tell her of their need to cut down expenses. "What can *I* do, Tertius?" is her question (ch. 58). Words, says the author, 'capable by varied vocal inflections of expressing all states of mind from helpless dimness to exhaustive argumentative perception, from the completest self-devoting fellowship to the most neutral aloofness'. Rosamond threw into the words 'as much neutrality as they could hold'. They fell like a mortal chill on Lydgate. Soon he found his resolution to sensible and honourable conduct 'beginning to relax under her torpedo-contact'. (It is perhaps unfortunate that the original sense of *torpedo*, a fish emitting a benumbing influence, has been covered over in modern usage by the explosive sense of the word – which suggests an influence quite the reverse of Rosamond's).

She is never to be convinced that her conduct has been less than admirable; she can follow no causes or effects except those that interest her; she can absolutely shut her eyes to facts and her ears to reason – and nothing will stop her from saying the same thing over and over again. She will even presume to advise Lydgate about his practice, which she has never troubled to understand. It is not surprising that he is angry. 'The shallowness of a water-nixie's soul may have a charm until she becomes didactic' (ch. 64), but not then.

She will lie, and countermand Lydgate's orders (to Trumbull, to let the house), and she will disobey him by writing to his uncle for money – when a personal application by himself might have been successful. It never occurs to her to help her husband in any way or to stand by him. When an inventory is to be made in the house for the security of the creditors, she wants to "go to papa's" (ch. 58). When a bailiff is put into the house, she retires to bed in blank despair. George Eliot drops into sentimentality over Lydgate and his dreadful plight. 'The strong man had had too much to bear that day. He let his head fall beside hers and sobbed' (ch. 59). There are other wives in Middlemarch with whom to compare her: Dorothea (as we have seen); Mrs Garth who produces her savings without a murmur to help Caleb (who has foolishly backed a bill of Fred's); and Mrs Bulstrode, who nobly stands by her husband in his disgrace. Lydgate could hardly have done worse for himself. When he appears to be involved in Bulstrode's disgrace, all Rosamond can see is that it is another argument for leaving Middlemarch (ch. 75).

And yet Lydgate is perhaps the tenderest husband in fiction, and more than any other has a conscience about the marriage bond. "There are things which husband and wife must think of together" (ch. 53). "We married because we loved each other, I suppose. And that may help us to pull along till things get better" (ch. 64). "You and I cannot have opposite interests. I cannot part my happiness from yours . . . When I hurt you, I hurt part of my own life" (ch. 65).

He had long ago given up the notion of her as the ideal wife, full of docile adoration: 'But the real wife had not only her claims, she had still a hold on his heart, and it was his desire that the hold should remain strong. In marriage the certainty, "She will never love me much", is easier to bear than the fear, "I shall love her no more" ' (ch. 64). Indeed, tired as he was, he was always most gentle to her; it was not through him that she was to come to her moment of truth.

She was 'one of those women who live much in the idea that each man they meet would have preferred them if the preference had not been hopeless' (ch. 75); and thus she learned her lesson.

She was flirting with Ladislaw, who seems to have felt himself in danger from her. As he wished to be an entirely honourable friend to Lydgate – for whom he had great sympathy – and as he cared for no woman but Dorothea, he attempted some sort of explanation. Dorothea suddenly came into the room, to see Rosamond with a 'flushed tearfulness' (ch. 77) and Ladislaw close to her, clasping 'both her upraised hands in his'. Not unnaturally she misunderstood the scene and retreated. Rosamond, believing in her power to soothe, laid her finger-tips on Ladislaw's sleeve. ' "Don't touch me!" he said, with an utterance like the threat of a lash' (ch. 78). In the scene that followed he told her some home-truths, the first that she is likely to have heard in her life.

Dorothea, who had intended to speak in defence of Lydgate, returned next day to perform her undone task. She, too, spoke of marriage seriously: Lydgate felt that his marriage was a bond that must affect his choice about everything – and therefore he hesitated to arrange to remain at the hospital. Then, with boldness, she spoke of the wrongness and hopelessness of love outside marriage. Rosamond, partly carried away by Dorothea's exaltation, clung to her and told her the truth. Will had not been making love to her on the previous day, but telling her that he loved another woman. That evening (ch. 82) she passed him a little note to tell him that the misunderstanding had been cleared up.

It would be agreeable to think that Rosamond was improved by this one generous moment – but unhappily moments of generosity do not seem to have such determining effects as moments of baseness; and evidently she had acted in Dorothea's strength rather than in her own. 'She simply continued to be mild in her temper, inflexible in her judgment, disposed to admonish her husband, and able to frustrate him by strategem' (Finale). Lydgate called her his basil plant, because it was a plant that had flourished wonderfully on a murdered man's brains.

The prelude is a mistake – it suggests that Dorothea is the most important character in *Middlemarch,* when at most she has primacy among several equals – also it emphasises too strongly one side of her nature.

Her religious point of view seems rather mixed up: she may have something of Emilia Strong's Anglo-Catholicism overlaid on George Eliot's early evangelicalism. She fasts 'like a Papist' (ch. 1) and knows passages of Pascal and Jeremy Taylor by heart – so did Emilia,[11] but Marian Evans received the *Pensées* of Pascal as a school-prize. Dorothea's ideas about dress seem rather puritanical, and education in Protestant Switzerland has left its mark on her. In short, she seems a good, pious, earnest young woman with no particular direction – and of course we first meet her two years or so before Keble's sermon on National Apostasy, and the beginning of the Oxford Movement.

[11] Betty Askwith, *Lady Dilke* (London 1969), p. 14.

Her spirituality is genuine, and Casaubon can understand her view of 'the secondary importance of ecclesiastical forms and articles of belief compared with that spiritual religion, that submergence of self in communion with Divine perfection which seemed to her to be expressed in the best Christian books' (ch. 3).

It is not she who misuses the word 'mysticism' in speaking of herself; it is Will Ladislaw (and 'mysticism' is the sort of word that journalists use unthinkingly). Dorothea has stated her belief: "That by desiring what is perfectly good, even when we don't quite know what it is and cannot do what we would, we are part of the divine power against evil – widening the skirts of light and making the struggle with darkness narrower" (ch. 39).

In fact she has only put into vague words the familiar teaching that we ought to unite our wills with the Divine Will.

"That is a beautiful mysticism," says Ladislaw – one has the uncomfortable suspicion that he is echoing George Eliot.

The comparison with St Teresa is particularly inept.

> O how oft shalt thou complain
> Of a sweet and subtle pain,
> Of intolerable joys;
> Of a death, in which who dies
> Loves his death, and dies again,
> And would for ever so be slain
> And lives, and dies; and knows not why
> To live, but that he still may die.

Crashaw's lines paraphrase closely a passage in the Saint's autobiography; George Eliot could not have begun to understand them. It is an inadequate apology to say that the comparison with St Teresa 'involves not mysticism, but the opportunity for practical work as the reformer of a religious order',[12] for all St Teresa's work as a foundress was directed towards fostering the life of prayer.

Dorothea felt she would have liked to marry 'the judicious Hooker', or Milton (ch. 1). Sometimes one is tempted to see in her a true niece of Arthur Brooke, for she has the same

[12] Haight *Biography*, p. 564.

habit of mental name-dropping. To her Casaubon seems 'a living Bossuet' or a 'modern Augustine'. If she marries him, 'it would be like marrying Pascal'. One may at least be glad that she did not think of marrying Bossuet (for it is certainly a wicked calumny of the duc de Richelieu's that he was secretly married), but it is hard to imagine how anyone who had attentively read the *Pensées* (and knew passages by heart) could think of Pascal as a marrying man.

Here one wonders how much the author is at fault. Dr Leavis thinks that George Eliot is doing some dangerous self-identification, particularly in such a passage as this: 'The intensity of her religious disposition, the coercion it exercised over her life, was but one aspect of a nature altogether ardent, theoretic, and intellectually consequent . . .' Nevertheless, there is a good deal of criticism of Dorothea.

Her temper was imperfect. When Sir James Chettam offered her a Maltese puppy: ' "It is painful to me to see these creatures that are bred merely as pets," said Dorothea, whose opinion was forming itself that very moment (as opinions will) under the heat of irritation' (ch. 3).

After a tiff with Celia: 'Dorothea was too much jarred to recover her temper and behave so as to show that she admitted any error in herself. She was disposed rather to accuse the intolerable narrowness and the purblind conscience of the society around her' (ch. 4).

Two small and unheroic points about her are made early in the book: she had caught 'a dramatic action' from Madame Poinçon, in whose house she had lived at Lausanne – Madame Poinçon might be a Protestant, but evidently she belonged to the Suisse romande. And (like Milly Barton) she was rather shortsighted.

Celia, moreover, who is certainly intended to be a most sympathetic character, is always there as a critic of Dorothea's 'notions' (ch. 3): after Casaubon's death she administered 'what she thought a sobering dose of fact. It was taking up notions that had done Dodo's health so much harm' (ch. 50), and Celia told her about Casaubon's codicil, to prevent her feeling any obligations towards her dead husband's wishes.

Two direct pieces of irony are also aimed at her. 'Mr Casaubon apparently did not care about building cottages, and

directed the talk to the extremely narrow accommodation
which was to be had in the dwellings of the ancient Egyptians,
as if to check too high a standard' (ch. 3). And when Dorothea
first visited Lowick, she found herself 'almost wishing that the
people needed more done for them' (ch. 9) – surely we are
meant to smile.

Lydgate thought her 'a little too serious' (ch. 10) when they
first met. "It is troublesome to talk to such women. They are
always wanting reasons, yet they are too ignorant to understand the merits of any question, and usually fall back on their
moral sense to settle things after their own taste." This is
certainly a criticism of Lydgate – who was to pay dearly for his
attraction towards a very different sort of woman – but it is
nevertheless a criticism of Dorothea.

Mrs Cadwallader has her own trenchant way of putting
things, but we need not altogether discount her view of
Dorothea, in whom she sees "a flighty sort of Methodistical
stuff" (ch. 6). She gives her remarkably sound advice in her
widowhood: ". . . Think what you might become yourself to
your fellow creatures if you were always playing tragedy
queen and taking things sublimely. Sitting alone in that
library at Lowick you may find yourself ruling the weather"
(ch. 54). If Romola had adopted the fancy of that unfortunate
character in Johnson's *Rasselas*, one may wonder who there
could have been to cure her of her delusion.

Dr Leavis suggests that Brooke's fatuousness disqualifies him
from serious comment. But when Dorothea says that the
great organ at Freiburg made her sob: "That kind of thing is
not healthy, my dear," says her uncle, and we are bound to
agree with him.

Dorothea's remarks or thoughts about art are nearly always
stupid or unsympathetic, but there she is probably not to be
separated from her author. The 'classical nudities and smirking
Renaissance-Corregiosities' (ch. 9) which her uncle brought
back to Tipton from his travels may not have been very successful copies of works of art, but need not have upset her as they
did. Pictures were a language that she could not understand
(here she was very unlike Emilia Pattison, who was a noted art
critic). Ladislaw was right to blame her for "fanaticism of
sympathy" when she was pained by "all this immense expense

of art, that seems somehow to lie outside life and make it no better for the world" (ch. 22). She used to come from the village "with all that dirt and coarse ugliness like a pain" (ch. 39) within her, and the "simpering pictures" in the drawing-room seemed to her "like a wicked attempt to find delight in what is false". We know Brooke is a bad landlord, and we have no reason to suppose him any better as a connoisseur – but there is no connection. Unhappily there is only too good reason to suppose that George Eliot sympathises with Dorothea, if we may judge from her remark about 'that softening influence of the fine arts which makes other people's hardships picturesque'.

Of course we may properly look at the countryside with the eyes of a social reformer or of a landscape artist, a Cobbett or a Gilpin; and we may change from one point of view to the other. It is, however, unwise and tactless to confuse the points of view. If we intrude on an account of human hardship with remarks about the picturesqueness of its setting, we shall be thought heartless or affected. If we intrude on other people's enthusiasm for a view with a melancholy account of human hardship, we shall appear priggish and puritanical (though people may lack the moral courage to tell us so). The fault is in each case the same: impatience and bad manners. There is (usually) time to think of everything in turn, and the two interests can be reconciled. We must not make people live in ill-drained cottages because they are pretty, nor must we erect an ill-designed charity institution in a beauty spot.

In her relations with Lydgate, when she is violently *exaltée* we find Dorothea difficult to accept. She is (as Dr Leavis says) presented as 'all-comprehending and irresistibly good'. He quotes: ' "Oh, it is bad!" said Dorothea. "I understand the difficulty there is in your vindicating yourself. And that all this should have come to you who had meant to lead a higher life than the common, and to find out better ways – I cannot bear to rest in this as unchangeable. I know you meant that. I remember what you said when you first spoke to me about the hospital. There is no sorrow I have thought about more than that – to love what is great, and to try to reach it, and yet to fail" ' (ch. 76).

But is all this 'winning simplicity' of Dorothea's quite the failure in touch that Dr Leavis believes? He reinforces his judgment by quoting Lydgate's words to himself: "This young creature has a heart large enough for the Virgin Mary. She evidently thinks nothing of her own future, and would pledge away half her income at once, as if she wanted nothing for herself but a chair to sit in from which she can look down with those clear eyes at the poor mortals who pray to her." This is dreadful – but in his emotion he may be *exalté* also, and we are not necessarily to see Dorothea through his eyes.

The question is, has George Eliot made her youthful self into Dorothea: no beauty, but far less unprepossessing than herself; no aristocrat, but undoubtedly a lady? Has she put her into a position of comparative wealth and influence, and are we to take her on her own valuation and Lydgate's? Or is this only part of the story – has she not also in her something of the fool who rushes in where angels fear to tread – a good-hearted, naive young woman (who is placed among very shrewd critics in Chapter 72) – but who blunderingly does, as such people sometimes will, do good? The latter interpretation fits the description of her at the beginning of the book: 'She was enamoured of intensity and greatness, and rash in embracing whatever seemed to her to have those aspects; likely to seek martyrdom, to make retractions, and then to incur martyrdom after all in a quarter where she had not sought it.'

We are told of her 'grand woman's frame' (ch. 79) being shaken by sobs – and it is an awkward echo of 'the strong man' (Lydgate, and also Adam Bede). But when Dorothea emerges from her night of agony, it is with very sensible feelings of duty towards three lives which she can, perhaps, set right: 'The objects of her rescue were not to be sought out by her fancy: they were chosen for her.'

'She opened her curtains, and looked out towards the bit of road that lay in view, with fields beyond, outside the entrance-gates. On the road there was a man with a burden on his back and a woman carrying her baby; in the field she could see figures moving – perhaps the shepherd with his dog . . . she was a part of that involuntary, palpitating life.' She was no madonna on her throne, but a part of the Homeric world, so full of men.

In her great scene with Rosamond, we are told of her

'nervous exaltation (ch. 81); she gets worked up in her ardour, but she has (as well she may) 'a dread upon her of presuming too far, and of speaking as if she herself were perfection addressing error'. All the same, Rosamond's generous effort is described as a 'reflex of her own energy' – and possibly Dorothea is still offered to us as an object of excessive veneration.

It has been suggested[13] that there is very little wrong with Dorothea as a character as long as Casaubon is alive, and that even after his death we can usually accept her, except in the scenes with Ladislaw; there she will not do, because Ladislaw will not do at all – in fact he is not there.

Will's father (Ladislaw II) was the son of a Polish patriot (Ladislaw I) and of Julia, sister to the mother of Edward Casaubon – who was disinherited because of this marriage. Will's mother was Sarah, daughter of that Mrs Dunkirk, who later became the first Mrs Bulstrode. Sarah ran away from home because she realised that her father's business was based on the receiving of stolen goods. Casaubon had traced his cousins, and had very generously paid for Will's rather haphazard studies.

Ironically, Will makes his second appearance to Dorothea (in Rome) as an unconscious reproach for her discontent, and a reminder of her husband's goodness (ch. 21); he has a happy way of drawing out Casaubon in conversation. It is also ironical that Casaubon should on several occasions insist that Will is not his nephew (he is his first cousin once removed); were he his nephew, he could never marry Dorothea.

Will is young and, apparently, attractive, with a 'ripple' in his nose (ch. 9). He stands for light, in opposition to Casaubon's darkness: he is 'lit up' with laughter, his smile was 'a gush of inward light, illuminating the transparent skin as well as the eyes' (ch. 21). For Dorothea 'the mere chance of seeing Will occasionally was like a lunette opened in the wall of her prison, giving her a glimpse of the sunny air' (ch. 37).

Possibly he is (in part) an idealisation of George Eliot's 'husband', George Henry Lewes. There is a drawing of Lewes in youth in which the face is charming; though Swinburne (outraged that Charlotte Brontë saw in him a likeness to her

---

[13] W. J. Harvey, *The Art of George Eliot* (London 1961), p. 191.

sister Emily) said that he was a vulgar little counter-jumper and even more hideous than his mistress, George Eliot. The description of their household as 'the fallen woman and the little dancing-master' is well known. Dorothea, of course, is not technically 'fallen'; but though her virtue is intact, she has fallen very low in the esteem of the good people of Freshitt and Tipton after her second marriage. They would hardly hesitate to use the term 'little dancing-master' of Ladislaw; they spoke of his grandfather, the Polish refugee, as 'an Italian with white mice'.

Brooke says (in his silly way): "Well, he may turn out a Byron, a Chatterton, a Churchill – that sort of thing" (ch. 9): that is, a poet. "He would make a good secretary now, like Hobbes, Milton, Swift – that sort of man" (ch. 34). He calls him "a kind of Shelley, you know . . . I don't mean as to anything objectionable – laxities or atheism, or anything of that kind, you know" (ch. 37), and he appears to him 'a sort of Burke with a leaven of Shelley' (ch. 51). Mrs Cadwallader thought him: "a sort of Byronic hero" (ch. 38).

Will has tried painting, and given it up; he turns to the political situation with equal enthusiasm, because Brooke is willing to employ him as an electioneering agent, and this keeps him near Dorothea – it is suggested that he has found work 'to take the place of dilettantism' (ch. 46) in writing for the *Pioneer*. He is slick, and has presence of mind and 'could find reasons impromptu, where he had not thought of a question beforehand' – not a very creditable gift, any more than Dorothea's of forming opinions under the heat of irritation. One cannot see that he displays much solidity of mind, or that his occupations are particularly worthy. Whatever view one might have taken of the political situation in England in 1831, one would be likely (like Lydgate) to think that it was useless to try to put Arthur Brooke into parliament.

After this he intends to go to London, and eat his dinners as a barrister, "since they say, that is the preparation for all public business" (ch. 54); and he aspires to do political work. We are not told how he is supporting himself at this time – but *Homo fictus* often seems to live upon air.

There is a strong attraction between him and Dorothea – but the language in which it is expressed is tiresomely winsome.

'Each looked at the other as if they had been two flowers which had opened then and there' (ch. 38).

'They were looking at each other like two fond children who were talking confidentially of birds' (ch. 39).

'She had turned her head and was looking out of the window on the rosebushes, which seemed to have in them the summers of all the years when Will would be away' (ch. 54).

It is, of course, possible that George Eliot thought this sort of language poetical. She was, in any case, nearly always shy of speaking about physical love (she had approached the subject most successfully when dealing with Stephen Guest and Maggie). Yet one wonders if she did not somehow incline to the opinion, held by Tipton and Freshitt, that Dorothea was throwing herself away – this grand soul captivated by a ripple in the curls and nose of a trivial young man. She certainly made an attempt to give weight to his personality, and to present him as an admirable husband, in contrast to Casaubon. This, however, could only be done at the (fairly reasonable) cost of Dorothea's ideals coming down a bit. She felt that there was 'always something better which she might have done, if she had only been better and known better' (Finale).

'No life would have been possible to Dorothea which was not filled with emotion . . . Will became an ardent public man, working well in those times when reforms were begun with a young hopefulness of immediate good which has been much checked in our days . . . Dorothea could have liked nothing better, since wrongs existed, than that her husband should be in the thick of a struggle against them, and that she should give him wifely help.'

That is vague enough. We are left thinking that Ladislaw was one of thousands of young men who have thought that they could change the world, but who are (at most) commemorated by a footnote in a blue book. George Eliot no longer had much faith in politics. Dorothea's 'wifely help' probably consisted in providing Will with a kind home, and holidays in Switzerland when he was run down; in copying papers for him, and pouring out coffee for his friends. 'No one stated exactly what else that was in her power she ought rather to have done' – in fact we end with a downgrading of Dorothea rather than with an upgrading of Ladislaw. They must have been, *mutatis mutandis*, rather like Mr Angus Wilson's 'darling dodos'.

Sir Leslie Stephen's comment, if unsympathetic, is very sensible: 'There was nothing for her to do; and I can only comfort myself by reflecting that, after all, she had a dash of stupidity, and that more successful Theresas may do a great deal of mischief.'

Caleb Garth is the ideal man of 'business' – by which he understands the business of a bailiff or overseer of landed property. In his integrity and devotion to his work he resembles Robert Evans, and is a more successful character derived from the author's father than Adam Bede.

Mary Garth has been too much admired. 'Her good sense, quick intelligence, and fine strength of character appear as the poised liveliness, shrewd good-humoured sharpness, and direct honesty of her speech': so wrote Dr Leavis. Some readers do not like her quite so much. She teases Fred, 'the corners of her mouth curling archly' (ch. 14), and she looks up at him 'with some roguishness'.

' "It is only that I have my girlish, mocking way of looking at things," said Mary with a returning playfulness in her answer which only made its modesty more charming' (ch. 52). Her heavy-footed charm is like that of a coy elephant; and her archness, roguishness and girlish mocking ways are quite as annoying as Dorothea's exaltation – and less excusable, because more fully conscious.

Mary herself has her moment of exaltation on the night of old Featherstone's death.

'He urged her to unlock his iron chest; there was not much time.

' "I cannot help that, sir. I will not let the close of your life soil the beginning of mine. I will not touch your iron chest or your will" ' (ch. 33).

The worst thing about this scene is that it is entirely futile. Had Mary obeyed Featherstone and destroyed his second will, his first must have been contested (since the existence of the second was known). This scene must be there because George Eliot admired it. It leads nowhere (in which it resembles the greater scene between Hetty and Dinah in *Adam Bede*). It might with advantage have been omitted from the book.

The little Garths are chiefly remarkable as another illustration of how very badly George Eliot does children's talk, and how stupidly she makes grown-up people talk to the young – with the exception of Mrs Garth, who is a teacher, and speaks to them in a common-sense way, both in that capacity and as their parent.

Nicholas Bulstrode was a charity schoolboy, who found himself taken up by the richer members of a Calvinistic dissenting church that he attended in Highbury. He married Mrs Dunkirk, widow of the richest of them, and was enriched by two frauds as a result of this marriage: the first fraud was that of her former husband, who had been more or less a 'fence'; the second was his own. He tacitly decided that Mrs Dunkirk's long missing daughter (now Sarah Ladislaw) should not be found, and she was not found. We meet him when he is the 'philanthropic banker' (ch. 10) of Middlemarch, already settled for many years in the town, and married to the mayor's sister, Harriet Vincy. He is predominant in the place, and many people are obliged to him for loans. He has left dissent in favour of the established Church ("as more genteel", says Raffles, and we may be sure that was the motive). He does a great deal of good in the town, where he is a patron of the new hospital. He is thinking of setting up as a country gentleman at Stone Court.

'There may be coarse hypocrites, who consciously affect beliefs and emotions for the sake of gulling the world, but Bulstrode was not one of them. He was simply a man whose desires had been stronger than his theoretical beliefs, and who had gradually explained the gratification of his desires into satisfactory agreement with those beliefs. If this be hypocrisy, it is a process which shows itself occasionally in us all . . .' (ch. 61). In short, Bulstrode is an example of Casuistry misapplied, or working upon false premises.

He believed 'that God intended him for special instrumentality'; he had always used money and position in the cause of religion, and had almost come to think that the blessings on his endeavours were a proof of their righteousness. Then Raffles appeared out of the past. Mrs Dunkirk had insisted on trying to find her lost daughter before she would make a second marriage. 'Bulstrode concurred; but after advertisement as well as other modes of inquiry had been tried, the mother believed that her daughter was not to be found, and consented to marry without reservation of property.'

The daughter had been found; but only one man besides Bulstrode knew it, and 'he was paid for keeping silence and carrying himself away'.

The man was Raffles. He appeared at Stone Court to dun Joshua Rigg (Featherstone's bastard son, and heir), for he had married Rigg's mother. Thus he re-entered Bulstrode's life as a blackmailer.

Bulstrode was safe from the Law, but he feared exposure, not only for the personal pain to himself and his wife, but also for the injury it would do to the cause of religion. 'What, if the acts he had reconciled himself to because they made him a stronger instrument of the divine glory, were to become the pretext of the scoffer, and a darkening of that glory?'

Fear drove him to attempt an act of restitution (and it was the fear of God, Who alone was to be placated). He offered money to Ladislaw, who rejected it with scorn (with too much scorn – for the offer touched him on a raw place, his own dignity).

Caleb, who refused to work any more with Bulstrode, rejected him with more compassion. "If you led a harmful life for gain, and kept others out of their rights by deceit, to get the more for yourself, I daresay you repent – you would like to go back, and can't: that must be a bitter thing. . . A man may do wrong, and his will may ride clear out of it, though he can't get his life clear. That's a bad punishment' (ch. 69).

This quiet charitableness of Caleb's forms an admirable contrast to Dorothea's emotional approach to Lydgate. Bulstrode has never been a sympathetic character. Like Lydgate (ch. 67) we have probably felt 'the strongest distaste for the broken metaphor and bad logic of the banker's religion'. Though publicly munificent, he has never been a generous man – we remember the meanness of his attitude to Fred Vincy's request for a letter denying that he has known him to trade on expectations from Featherstone. His unattractive, puritanical Evangelicalism is one of the forces that darken English provincial life – the Vincys are exceptional in Middlemarch, because they have a cheerful house, and are not afraid to enjoy themselves.

Bulstrode, as Vincy bears witness, is a real believer: "a man who half starves himself, and goes the length in family prayers, and so on, that you do, believes in his religion" (ch. 13).

In a sad way, we can believe that Bulstrode has a higher vocation to virtue than an ordinary man like Vincy, though he is stained with worse sins. George Eliot exercises the same delicate moral judgment here as when she showed us that Maggie Tulliver, in the wrong, might be better than Tom in the right. Bulstrode is no Tartuffe or Pecksniff – and though the base of his fortune is fraudulent (and restitution must now in most cases be impossible) he has more than twenty years of honourable life behind him.

The death of Raffles is a wonderful contrivance.

'I think,' Ivy Compton-Burnett said, 'there are signs that strange things happen, though they do not emerge. I believe that it would go ill with many of us if we were faced with a strong temptation, and I suspect that with some of us it does go ill.'[14]

The black-mailer was in his hands, sick, at Stone Court. Lydgate ordered a strict absention from alcohol. Bulstrode carried out his orders, though Raffles pleaded for brandy, and the housekeeper begged to be allowed to give it him. Bulstrode could not be *sure* that Lydgate was right – most other doctors would have advocated a different treatment. He weakened, and gave his housekeeper the key to the cellar. The situation is rich in opportunities for casuistry; and even if it should be discovered that Lydgate's orders were disobeyed there could be no basis for a criminal charge. We know (however) that if Bulstrode had wished the sick man to recover, he would have trusted Lydgate's medical knowledge. Nevertheless, he was in a muddle – muddle, the result of sin (which destroys order) as well as its cause. He was quite sincere in repenting of his later sins as hypothetical, 'hypothetically praying for their pardon: "if I have herein transgressed" ' (ch. 71).

The finest behaviour in the whole book is that of Mrs Bulstrode, after her husband's disgrace.

'She locked herself in her room. She needed time to get used to her maimed consciousness, her poor lopped life, before she

[14] Conversation with Margaret Jourdain.

could walk steadily to the place allotted to her. A new searching
light had fallen on her husband's character, and she could not
judge him leniently: the twenty years in which she had
believed in him and venerated him by virtue of his conceal-
ments came back with particulars that made them seem an
odious deceit. . . But this imperfectly taught woman, whose
phrases and habits were an odd patchwork, had a loyal spirit
within her. The man whose prosperity she had shared through
nearly half a life, and who had unvaryingly cherished her –
now that punishment had befallen him, it was not possible to
her in any sense to forsake him. There is a forsaking which still
sits at the same board and lies on the same couch with the
forsaken soul, withering it the more by unloving proximity
[cf. Mrs Bulstrode's niece, Rosamond]. She knew, when she
locked her door, that she should unlock it, ready to go down to
her unhappy husband and espouse his sorrow, and say of his
guilt, I will mourn and not reproach. But she needed time to
gather up her strength; she needed to sob out her farewell to all
the gladness and pride of her life' (ch. 74). Dorothea was to
put on lighter mourning and a new bonnet to encourage her
on her great visit to Rosamond; Mrs Bulstrode put on a plain
black gown to go down in mercy to her husband.

'A movement of new compassion and old tenderness went
through her like a great wave, and putting one hand on his
which rested on the arm of the chair, and the other on his
shoulder, she said, solemnly but kindly –

' "Look up, Nicholas." '

Middlemarch itself, with its county surroundings at Freshitt,
Tipton and Lowick, is the real subject of the book. Sometimes
the connections between the inhabitants are too closely drawn.
Eighteen of the principal characters (all except the Farebrothers and Cadwalladers) are linked by a continuous chain
of kindred and affinity, which, despite class differences,
connects not only local characters but also (more improbably)
characters whose origins are not in or near Middlemarch, such
as Ladislaw, Bulstrode and Raffles (see pp. 160-1).

Threads of interest as well as those of family draw people
together – we saw the pressure on Lydgate at the time of the
voting on the chaplaincy. Gossip is potent – and we find

innocent Fred Vincy scattering it as carelessly as a bee sheds pollen. He went to Lowick parsonage to see Mary Garth, and picked up from Henrietta Noble (Farebrother's aunt) the story of Casaubon's will: their servant had got it from Dorothea's maid. Fred passed it on, as a piece of indifferent news, to Rosamond – and thence (despite Lydgate's warning to her) it got to Will.

Moreover, there is 'Candour'. In Jane Austen's novels 'Candour' means believing the best of people as far as one can. 'To be candid in Middlemarch phraseology meant, to use an early opportunity of letting your friends know that you did not take a cheerful view of their capacity, their conduct or their position; and a robust candour never waited to be asked its opinion' (ch. 74). A wife, therefore, could not long remain ignorant that the town held a bad opinion of her husband.

Mrs Plymdale is a minor character – though she was instrumental in causing Lydgate's engagement to Rosamond. Her later dilemma illustrates the pressure of Middlemarch. She is a personal friend of Mrs Bulstrode's, and the Plymdale dyeing house has a profitable connection with the banker. On the other hand, her son Ned (Rosamond's former suitor) is to be married – perhaps is already married – to Sophy Toller, who belongs to the 'best circle' in the town, from a social point of view. Mrs Bulstrode, however, shares with her the 'serious view' which she thinks 'best' in another sense. 'The sharp little woman's conscience was somewhat troubled in the adjustment of these opposing "bests".' We can laugh at her without compassion, and she provides comic relief in the pathetic story of Mrs Bulstrode.

Apart from the interrelation of characters by blood or marriage or business, and from the influence that they exert on one another's lives by gossip, there are formal patterns and contrasts between themes and characters that play a large part in the design of the book.

Casaubon's learned but futile studies which at first attract Dorothea, are paralleled by Lydgate's promising research, which means nothing to Rosamond. They are parodied in Brooke's absurd documents – and Will becomes his assistant to be near Dorothea. Featherstone's will, which disturbs but does not separate Fred and Mary, is paralleled by that of Casaubon,

which is intended to separate Will and Dorothea, but has no
such effect. Featherstone and Bulstrode are both money-
makers, but Bulstrode tries to do good, and Featherstone
merely to cause annoyance. Caleb Garth, who would wrong no
man, even if he knew that God winked at it, is a contrast to
Bulstrode, who so greatly hopes that God will overlook the
wrong that he has done. Fred, who refuses to go into the
Church without vocation, contrasts with Camden Farebrother
who has gone into the Church without vocation. They are both
in love with Mary. It has been rightly observed[15] that this last
triangle shows 'too obviously the contriving and manipulating
hand of the artist anxious to inject a little drama into even the
most subsidiary of her situations'.

The same critic observes: 'The syntactical evolution of her
sentences is thoroughly intellectual. The lengthy and sometimes cumbrous accumulation of parenthesis and qualifying
clauses is the correlative of a cerebral talent concerned to
analyse and scrutinise closely the moral and emotional
intricacies of her characters.' He compares it with that of Dr
Johnson, quoting Dr Leavis' judgment of the latter, that he
was able 'to give his moral declamation the weight of lived
experience and transform his eighteenth-century generalities
into that extraordinary kind of concreteness'. Certainly the
best parts of her analysis are felt to advance the creation of her
characters and of her world.

We have been warned by several critics against applying the
canons of Henry James to pre-Jamesian fiction. Nevertheless
many of us have been so conditioned by him to feel the necessity
of representation, and the superiority of scene over summary
that for us (as for him) 'the novelist who doesn't represent and
represent all the time is lost'. Even if we approach *Middlemarch*
from this point of view, we can yet justify the better pages of
analysis – they are nearly always fusions of summary and scene.

Not only are such passages often strongly visual, they are also
full of interior dialogue, and not infrequently of the reported
comments of the world of Middlemarch. Some of these elements
are present in an early description of Bulstrode.

'The banker's speech was fluent, but it was also copious, and

---

[15] Harvey, p. 142.

he used up an appreciable amount of time in brief meditative pauses. Do not imagine his sickly aspect to have been of the yellow, black-haired sort: he had a pale blond skin, thin grey-besprinkled brown hair, light grey eyes and a large forehead. Loud men called his subdued tone an undertone, and some-times implied that it was inconsistent with openness; (though there seems no reason why a loud man should not be given to concealment of anything except his own voice unless it can be shown that Holy Writ has placed the seat of candour in the lungs.) Mr Bulstrode had also a deferential bending attitude in listening, and an apparently fixed attentiveness in his eyes which made those persons who thought themselves worth hearing infer that he was seeking the utmost improvement from their discourse' (ch. 13).

Here we can see and hear Bulstrode, hear even the pauses in his speech, hear what others said and even what they thought about him, though we could do without the facetious concessive clause, here bracketed.

Many passages of interior monologue put (e.g.) into Casau-bon's mind, are felt as speech just as much as if they had been pronounced.

Other passages of summarised thought make us feel that we are watching the thinker, who suddenly comes out with a few words at intervals – they almost anticipate the monologue with closed lips on the cinema.

'When he was gone, Rosamond left her chair and walked to the other end of the room, leaning when she got there against a *chiffonière*, and looking out of the window wearily. She was oppressed by ennui, and by that dissatisfaction which in women's minds is continually turning into a trival jealousy, referring to moral claims, springing from no deeper passion than the vague exactingness of egoism, and yet capable of impelling action as well as speech. "There is really nothing to care for much," said poor Rosamond inwardly, thinking of the family at Quallingham, who did not write to her; and that perhaps Tertius when he came home would tease her about expenses' (ch. 69).

The interior monologue of Bulstrode's temptation, with all its movement of hopes and fears, evil promptings and resistance, is surely representation.

'His mind was crowded with images and conjectures, which were a language to his hopes and fears, just as we hear tones from the vibrations which shake our whole system. The deep humiliation with which he winced under Caleb Garth's knowledge of his past and rejection of his patronage, alternated and almost gave way to the sense of safety in the fact that Garth and no other had been the man to whom Raffles had spoken. It seemed to him a sort of earnest that Providence intended his rescue from worse consequences; the way being thus open for the hope of secrecy. That Raffles should be afflicted with illness, that he should have been led to Stone Court rather than elsewhere – Bulstrode's heart fluttered at the vision of probabilities which these events conjured up. If it should turn out that he was freed from all danger of disgrace – if he could breathe in perfect liberty – his life should be more consecrated than it had ever been before. He mentally lifted up this vow as if it would urge the result he longed for – he tried to believe in the potency of that prayerful resolution – its potency to determine death. He knew that he ought to say, "Thy will be done"; and he said it often. But the intense desire remained that the will of God might be the death of that hated man' (ch. 69).

The dialogue is generally so good that one may regret that there is not more of it. The best talk is often that of the lighter characters, who bring a freshness and even a welcome frivolity into the atmosphere. The charming staccato voice of Celia often deflates the solemnity of Dorothea, and Arthur Brooke's engaging silliness is a corrective to the overearnestness of Casaubon. Minor characters like Mrs Cadwallader, Mrs Plymdale, Mrs Waule and the amusing auctioneer Trumbull all make their mark every time they speak.

Rosamond can hardly open her mouth without giving herself away; she is admirably mocked and played with by her brother Fred (ch. 11), and almost as well brought out by Mary (ch. 12) – though Mary, more of a favourite with the author than she is likely to be with the reader, is herself arch and tiresome.

The great and sincere speech forced out of Rosamond by Dorothea's own virtue is in a toneless, strained, accurately truthful 'Basic English' which recalls (as it may have influenced) some of the greatest scenes of Ivy Compton-Burnett.

' "He was telling me how he loved another woman, that I might know he could never love me," said Rosamond, getting more and more hurried as she went on. "And now I think he hates me because – because you mistook him yesterday. He says it is through me that you will think ill of him – think that he is a false person. But it shall not be through me. He has never had any love for me – I know he has not – he has always thought slightly of me. He said yesterday that no other woman existed for him beside you. The blame of what happened yesterday is entirely mine. He said he could never explain to you – because of me. He said you could never think well of him again. But now I have told you, and he cannot reproach me any more" ' (ch. 81).

In a book so closely knit together it was hardly necessary to add the additional binding force of imagery, and that of the 'web' is overdone, though in itself a natural enough image.

'I at least have so much to do in unravelling certain human lots', says the author, 'and seeing how they were woven and interwoven, that all the light I can command must be concentrated on this particular web' (ch. 15).

'Municipal town and rural parish gradually made fresh threads of connection' (ch. 11) at the time of the story. Lydgate was feeling (by an odd mixture of metaphor) 'the hampering threadlike pressure of small social conditions and their frustrating complexity' (ch. 18). He was to say, of Farebrother, "There are so many strings pulling at once" (ch. 50).

The web of love-making or mutual attraction is more precisely called a spider's web. 'Has anyone ever pinched into its pilulous smallness the cobweb of pre-matrimonial acquaintanceship?' (ch. 2). This hideous phrase is devoted to Dorothea, but the great spinner of webs is Rosamond. Ever since Lydgate's arrival 'she had woven a little future' (ch. 12), though he had not been 'weaving any future in which their lots were united' (ch. 13).

It is to their 'mutual web' that some of the most tasteless writing in the book is devoted. 'Young love-making – that gossamer web! Even the points it clings to – the things whence its subtle interlacings are swung – are scarcely perceptible:

momentary touches of finger tips, meeting of rays from blue
and dark orbs, unfinished phrases, lightest changes of cheek
and lips, faintest tremors. The web itself is made of spontaneous
beliefs and indefinable joys, yearnings of one life towards
another, visions of completeness, indefinite trust. And Lydgate
fell to spinning that web from his inward self with wonderful
rapidity. . . As for Rosamond, she was in the water-lily's
expanding wonderment at its own fuller life, and she was
spinning industriously at the mutual web' (ch. 36). Here is a
lily, most unscripturally engaged in spinning.

The web, however, was not only spun by lovers. Bulstrode
had been spinning his self-justifying arguments 'into intricate
thickness, like masses of spider-web, padding the moral
sensibility' (ch. 61). And in Casaubon 'suspicion and jealousy
. . . were constantly at their weaving work' (ch. 42).

The book abounds, more than any other of this author's, in
imagery that verges on the grotesque. There is, in particular, a
very strange use of myth.

'Poor Rosamond lost her appetite and felt as forlorn as
Ariadne – as a charming stage Ariadne left behind with her
boxes of costumes and no hope of a coach' (ch. 31). A coach
would be of little use on Naxos, to follow Theseus' 'perjured sails'.

'Rosamond Vincy appeared to be that perfect piece of
womanhood who would reverence her husband's mind after
the fashion of an accomplished mermaid, using her comb and
looking-glass, and singing her song for the relaxation of his
adored wisdom alone' (ch. 58). That is not how the mermaid
of legend behaves – who would be no bad image of Rosamond,
for she is the sailor's destruction.

The scientific metaphors are no happier.

'Celia's face had the shadow of a pouting expression on it,
the full presence of the pout being kept back by an habitual
awe of Dorothea and principle; two associated facts which
might show a mysterious electricity if you touched them
incautiously' (ch. 1).

The 'pedantic' or 'polysyllabic' humour has in no way
diminished since the Clerical Scenes.

'Domestic reality met them in the shape of uncles' (Prelude).

'In fact, if that convenient vehicle had existed in the days of
the Seven Sages, one of them would doubtless have remarked

that you can know little of women by following them about in their pony-chaises' (ch. 6).

'In fact, the world is full of hopeful analogies and handsome dubious eggs called possibilities' (ch. 10).

'When the animals entered the ark in pairs, one may imagine that allied species made much private remark on each other and were tempted to think that so many forms feeding on the same fodder were eminently superfluous, as tending to diminish the rations' (ch. 35).

'He did not shrug his shoulders; and for want of that muscular outlet he thought more irritably of beautiful lips kissing holy skulls and other emptinesses ecclesiastically enshrined' (ch. 37).

The book is disfigured by a quantity of references and quotations of an oddness or pretentiousness which perhaps originate in the author's autodidactism; she never learned the sort of literary tact which avoids them.

'A learned provincial clergyman is accustomed to think of his acquaintance as of "lords, knyghtes, and other noble and worthi men, that conne Latyn but little" ' (ch. 3).

'In fact, much the same sort of movement and mixture went on in old England, as we find in older Herodotus, who also, telling what had been, thought it well to take a woman's lot for his starting-point, though Io, as a maiden apparently beguiled by attractive merchandise, was the reverse of Miss Brooke. . .' (ch. 11).

'Is it due to excess of poetry or stupidity that we are never weary of describing what King James called a woman's "makdom and her fairness"?' (ch. 15).

'Even couplets from Pope may be but "fallings from us, vanishings" when fear clutches us, and a glass of sherry is hurrying like smoke among our ideas' (ch. 51).

'He was squinting as if he did it with design, like the gipsies when Borrow read the New Testament to them' (ch. 32).

'For he was not one of these gentlemen who languish after the unattainable Sappho's apple that laughs from the topmost bough' (ch. 6).

'Solomon's Proverbs, I think, have omitted to say, that as the sore palate findeth grit, so an uneasy conscience heareth innuendos' (ch. 31).

One may conclude this catalogue of horrors with a 'quotation-sandwich'.

'Pity, that "new born babe" which was by-and-by to rule many a storm within her, did not "stride the blast" on this occasion' (ch. 29).

There is probably no novel so fine as *Middlemarch* that contains so much bad and tasteless writing. It illustrates two

A TABLE OF KINDRED A

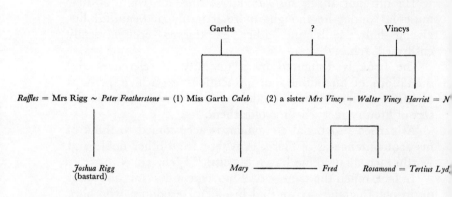

THE RELATIONSHIPS IN 'MIDDLEMARCH'

It will be seen from the above table that eighteen of the principal characters are linked in a continuous chain of kindred and affinity; only the Farebrothers and the Cadwalladers are omitted.

BROOKE, Arthur. Uncle to Dorothea and Celia

BROOKE, Celia. Niece to Arthur, sister to Dorothea, wife to Sir James Chettam, sister-in-law to Edward Casaubon and Will Ladislaw

BROOKE, Dorothea. Niece to Arthur, sister to Celia, wife (successively) to Edward Casaubon and Will Ladislaw

BULSTRODE, Harriet. Sister to Walter Vincy, aunt to Fred and Rosamond Vincy, wife to Nicholas Bulstrode, aunt-by-marriage to Tertius Lydgate

BULSTRODE, Nicholas. Step-grandfather to Will Ladislaw, husband to Harriet, brother-in-law to Walter Vincy, uncle-by-marriage to Fred and Rosamond Vincy

CASAUBON, Edward. Husband to Dorothea, brother-in-law to Celia, first-cousin-once-removed to Will Ladislaw

CHETTAM, Sir James. Husband to Celia, brother-in-law to Dorothea

FEATHERSTONE, Peter. Uncle-by-marriage to Mary Garth,

truths, neither of which is very popular with some critics: that autodicacticism will not take the place of instilled or inherited culture, and that books are not written with words alone. If we were to judge George Eliot by the way in which she uses words she might take a very low place, less high, probably, than the late Dorothy Sayers.

FFINITY IN MIDDLEMARCH

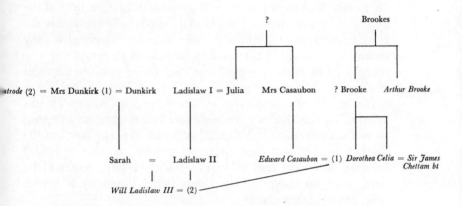

and to Fred and Rosamond Vincy; father to Joshua Rigg (bastard)

GARTH, Caleb. Brother-in-law to Featherstone, father to Mary, father-in-law to Fred

GARTH, Mary. Daughter to Caleb, niece-by-marriage to Featherstone, wife to Fred

LADISLAW III, Will. Step-grandson to Bulstrode, first-cousin-once-removed to Casaubon, husband to Dorothea

LYDGATE, Tertius. Husband to Rosamond, son-in-law to Vincy, brother-in-law to Fred, nephew by-marriage to Mrs Bulstrode

RAFFLES. Stepfather to Joshua Rigg

RIGG, Joshua. Bastard son of Peter Featherstone, stepson to Raffles

VINCY, Fred. Son to Walter, brother to Rosamond, husband to Mary, nephew to Mrs Bulstrode, nephew-by-marriage to Peter Featherstone and to Bulstrode, brother-in-law to Tertius Lydgate

VINCY, Mrs. Wife to Walter, mother to Fred and Rosamond, sister-in-law to Featherstone and to Mrs Bulstrode, mother-in-law to Tertius Lydgate

VINCY, Walter. Father of Fred and Rosamond, brother-in-law of Bulstrode, brother of Mrs Bulstrode, father-in-law of Lydgate and Mary

VIII   Daniel Deronda

'As for the bad part, there *is* nothing to do but cut it away,' said Dr Leavis, and most readers will agree with him, in spite of the author. She was tired of 'the laudation of readers who cut the book into scraps and talk of nothing in it but Gwendolen'; she meant 'everything in the book to be related to everything else there'.[1] Most authors would like that to be possible for their books.

No doubt she preferred to attribute the failure of this relation to the reader's insensibility, rather than to her own lack of artistry, even to his racial or religious prejudice: but the English reader had long been accustomed to love a Jewish heroine, Rebecca, and to hate a Jewish villain, Shylock; he need have no compunction about being bored by a Jewish prig, Daniel Deronda.

Even the fact that Deronda could not get much satisfaction out of the system of education at Cambridge – which slightly commends him, or the author's presentation of him, to Dr Leavis – is not really in his favour (ch. 16). His was not the creative mind for which set studies are unfit, and it may be feared that he inclined rather 'to go and study abroad' – that is, to research, rather than to seek culture.

His pomposity is not only exhibited in his 'spiritual advice' to Gwendolen, but is present as a fault in tone, even when what he has to say is sensible enough.

' "For my part", said Deronda, "people who do anything finely always inspirit me to try. I don't mean that they make me believe that I can do it as well. But they make the thing, whatever it may be, seem worthy to be done. I can bear to think my own music not good for much, but the world would

[1] Haight *Letters*, VI, p. 290.

be dismal if I thought music itself not good for much. Excellence encourages one about life generally; it shows the spiritual wealth of the world."

' "But then, if we can't imitate it, it only makes our own life seem the tamer," said Gwendolen, in a mood to resent encouragement founded on her own insignificance.

' "That depends on the point of view, I think," said Deronda. "We should have a poor life of it if we were reduced to our own performances. A little private imitation of what is good is a sort of private devotion to it, and most of us ought to practise art only in the light of private study-preparation to understand and enjoy what the few can do for us" ' (ch. 35).

This last speech is important to the structure of the novel and the relation of one part to the other. The theme of singing faintly echoes through the book.

Daniel, as we shall learn, was the son of a great singer Alcharisi, and the legitimate issue of her husband – both were Jews. She had disliked her Jewish education and had given up her religion. She believed that they would be a disadvantage to her son, and she handed him over to be brought up as an English gentleman by one of her admirers, Sir Hugo Mallinger. Sir Hugo once asked him if he would care to become a singer, and he was distressed, for it seemed like a reflection on his birth. He believed that he was Sir Hugo's bastard son, and was anxious not to lose caste further. And it may be said that to be the bastard of a man so excellent and so rich as Sir Hugo was no sorry position; Alcharisi had not chosen badly for her son, and might fairly expect no censure except from strict Jews for depriving him of his 'birthright'. It was unfortunate for her that Daniel felt otherwise.

For he had fallen in love with Mirah, a Jewish girl, an exquisite singer, though her voice was not strong enough for the stage. He had hunted for her long lost brother Mordecai, and had found him. With Mordecai as his tutor he had become more and more fascinated by the History and Culture of the Hebrews, and when he learned of his own Jewish origins he was filled with joy: now he had a mission, to help his people to found a home of their own in Palestine. He married Mirah under the velvet canopy. 'Sir Hugo and Lady Mallinger had taken trouble to provide a complete equipment for Eastern travel': one envisages mosquito nets, sola topis, and elaborate picnic baskets with spirit lamps.

This part of the story has only to be stated to seem *outré* and even comic, and for all George Eliot's generous and intelligent interest in the Jewish people it is hard to believe that it did them much good. Mordecai is as intolerable as Daniel, and his story and Mirah's is further weighted down by the presence of an insufferable family of Aryan bores, the Meyricks.

One may rejoice to concur with Dr Leavis (in many respects the best critic of George Eliot) that it is not the author's intellect that is to blame for the 'bad part' of the book, for it is more marked by emotionalism than cerebration. Daniel is another of George Eliot's idealised and idealistic *personae*, in the line of Maggie Tulliver and Dorothea Casaubon. The Jewish part is not (as Henry James complained) 'at bottom cold'; it leaves the reader cold, but it must have been written with ardour.

The faint echo of singing connects it with the other part of the book. Gwendolen would like to be a singer when her family has lost its money, but it is too late for her to start on that arduous career – for which she has, in any case, no vocation. Moreover we can agree with Constantius in Henry James's dialogue about this book that: 'Her finding Deronda pre-engaged to go to the East and stir up the race-feeling of the Jews strikes me as a wonderfully happy invention. The irony of the situation for poor Gwendolen is almost grotesque.' We cannot quite wonder with him whether 'the whole heavy structure of the Jewish question in the story was not built up by the author for the express purpose of giving its proper force to this particular stroke' – we know that the author took it far too seriously – but we are content to value it for this effect.

The first thing to be said about the good part of *Daniel Deronda* is that the writing is infinitely better than in *Middlemarch*. Clumsiness and tortuousness of expression are not wanting, but are far less frequent; and happily there is no pattern of imagery.

Henry James' great interest in this part of *Daniel Deronda* is proved by his dialogue. Dr Leavis believed that it inspired him to make another picture of an unhappy marriage in *The Portrait of a Lady*.

It must at once be obvious that the fable is very different, whatever we may think of the similarity of the heroine. Isabel is an orphaned American girl: she has lately lost a most devoted father, but Henry James seems to give contradictory dates for her mother's death. Mrs Touchett telegraphs: 'Taken sister's child, died last year, go to Europe.'[2] But Isabel says to her cousin Ralph: 'There had been some disagreements between your mother and my father, after my mother's death, which took place when I was a child.'[3] Isabel has two married sisters, from one of whom her aunt, Mrs Touchett, takes her to Europe.

Gwendolen, whose father (apparently a man of good family) has died some years ago, goes to England with her mother, Mrs Davilow, and her four young half-sisters on the death of the unsatisfactory step-father. They settle in a small country house to be near Fanny Davilow's married sister and her husband, Henry Gascoigne, the rector.

As in some much earlier novels, there is this much likeness in the stories that we see two young women entering English county society. Both of them do it from the fringe: Isabel from the house of an expatriate American uncle and his largely absentee wife; Gwendolen introduced by the rectory.

Both of them are striking young women, though Gwendolen's appeal is mainly to the eye, and Isabel's to the intellect. We are told of Gwendolen: 'Perhaps it would have been rash to say that she was at all exceptional inwardly, or that the unusual in her was more than her grace of movement and bearing' (ch. 6). Both have the charm of novelty in their surroundings: each of them receives a proposal of marriage from the most eligible bachelor in the neighbourhood: Isabel from Lord Warburton, and Gwendolen from Henleigh Mallinger Grandcourt – who is likely to inherit both a baronetcy and a peerage.

Both girls are portionless, but Isabel has an American independence, and no doubt feels that her aunt will not leave

2 *Portrait of a Lady*, ch. 1.
3 ibid, ch. 5.

her to fend for herself. Gwendolen, on the contrary, has a
family to think of and to think for her. Neither is in love;
Isabel rejects Lord Warburton because she wants to keep her
liberty for a time, Gwendolen is much inclined to accept
Grandcourt.

Her uncle, Henry Gascoigne, her only male adviser, was very
much in favour. 'This match with Grandcourt presented itself
to him as a sort of public affair; perhaps there were ways in
which it might even strengthen the establishment. To the
rector, whose father (nobody would have suspected it, and
nobody was told) had risen to be a provincial corn-dealer,
aristocratic heirship resembled regal heirship in excepting its
possessor from the ordinary standard of moral judgments.
Grandcourt, the almost certain baronet, the probable peer, was
to be ranged with public personages, and was a match to be
accepted on broad general grounds national and ecclesiastical
. . . if Grandcourt had really made any deeper or more unfortunate experiments in folly than were common in young
men of high prospects, he was of an age to have finished with
them. All accounts can be suitably wound up when a man has
not ruined himself, and the expense may be taken as insurance
against future error' (ch. 13).

Thus far the 'practical wisdom' of the good, worldly rector;
he had heard vague rumours about Grandcourt, but supposed
he was now such that 'a woman of well-regulated mind' could
be happy with him. Gwendolen was very much inclined to
follow his advice, until her meeting with Grandcourt's former
mistress.

Lydia Glasher is a character out of Balzac. She had left her
husband (and a child who died soon after) for Grandcourt, to
whom she bore four children. Her husband was now dead, and
she hoped that Grandcourt would marry her and make her
boy his heir (ch. 30). Meanwhile she was living at Gadsmere,
'a rambling, patchy house' in the coal country, in a seclusion
that protected her from curiosity; her life was bound up with
her children.

Lush, Grandcourt's factotum and former tutor, was Lydia's
ally, and had a strong dislike for Gwendolen (which was fully
returned); he contrived an encounter between the two women
at an archery meeting. Gwendolen now felt that she could not

marry Grandcourt, and she at once went abroad with her friends the Langens.

It was while travelling with them that she visited the gaming-tables at Leubronn, and there the reader first sees her, in the opening chapter of the book. It was there, probably, that George Eliot first saw her.

She wrote (from Homburg): 'I am not fond of denouncing my fellow-sinners, but gambling being a vice I have no mind to, it stirs my disgust even more than my pity. The sight of the dull faces bending round the gaming tables, the raking-up of the money, and the flinging of the coins towards the winners by the hard-faced croupiers, the hateful, hideous women staring at the board like stupid monomaniacs – all this seems to me the most abject presentation of mortals grasping after something called a good that can be seen on the face of this little earth . . . Hell is the only right name for such places.'[4] A few days later (4 October 1872) she was writing from the same place: 'There is very little dramatic "stuff" to be picked up by watching or listening. The saddest thing to be witnessed is the play of Miss Leigh, Byron's grand niece, who is only twenty-six years old, and is completely in the grasp of this mean, money-making demon. It made me cry to see her young fresh face among the hags and brutally stupid men around her.'[5]

Daniel Deronda, looking on, puts the evil eye on Gwendolen (as she thinks); they are not yet acquainted. When she sells her turquoise necklace with anonymous impertinence he buys it back and returns it to her. Later he becomes to her a symbol of the truth that one man's gain is another man's loss. The gaming-table had already shown her that; but she believed that he was Sir Hugo Mallinger's bastard son – and that it was by reason of his wrongs that Grandcourt was Sir Hugo's heir. It would therefore be doubly wrong to marry Grandcourt – Deronda would be further cut out from the Mallinger estates, and Mrs Glasher's family from the rest of Grandcourt's property.

Isabel, on the contrary, has nothing Byronic about her, and nothing of the 'Lamia beauty' (ch. 1) of Gwendolen. It is hard

[4] Haight *Letters*, v, p. 312.
[5] ibid., p. 314.

to imagine her at the gaming table. She never has Gwendolen's temptation to profit by another's loss.

Gwendolen is called home by the financial ruin of her family. It might almost be thought that Henry James deliberately reversed the situation for Isabel, for her uncle is persuaded by his son, Ralph, to leave her seventy thousand pounds. She faces the world, rich and independent; while Gwendolen is faced with the prospect of going as governess to the Bishop's Palace.

She makes one pathetic attempt to escape. She sees Herr Klesmer, a noted musician staying in the neighbourhood, to ask if there is any hope of her being able to earn her living on the stage. Klesmer teaches her the painful lesson that Henry James's Monarchs have to learn in *The Real Right Thing*: "Ladies and gentlemen think that when they have made their toilet and drawn off their gloves they are as presentable on the stage as in a drawing-room. No manager thinks that" (ch. 23). Isabel has no histrionic talents or ambitions.

There is now a likelihood, almost a certainty, that Grandcourt will repeat his offer, and Gwendolen undergoes that temptation that so often, in one way or another, has been the lot of George Eliot's characters from Arthur Donnithorne to Bulstrode.

'Through the last twenty hours, with a brief interruption of sleep, she had been so occupied with perpetually alternating images and arguments for and against the possibility of her marrying Grandcourt, that the conclusion which she had determined on beforehand ceased to have any hold on her consciousness: the alternative dip of counterbalancing thoughts begotten of counterbalancing desires had brought her into a state in which no conclusion could look fixed to her. She would have expressed her resolve as before; but it was a form out of which the blood had been sucked – no more a part of quivering life than the "God's will be done" of one who is eagerly watching chances. She did not mean to accept Grandcourt; from the first moment of receiving his letter she had meant to refuse him; still that could not but prompt her to look the unwelcome reasons full in the face until she had a little less awe of them, and could not hinder her imagination from filling out her knowledge in various ways, some of which seemed to change the aspect of what she knew. By dint of looking at a dubious object with constructive imagination, who cannot give it twenty different shapes?' (ch. 27).

Gwendolen has, as Isabel has not, a moral conflict: her story briefly analysed (as we have been taught to do) in words that would fit on the back of a postcard, would read as follows: 'Striking girl tempted by poverty into unsuitable marriage, at expense of another's claim; subsequent punishment.'

She has yielded to temptation and taken what was another's, like Arthur Donnithorne (though he knew nothing of Adam's claim), like Maggie Tulliver, like Tito, like Mrs Transome and like Bulstrode. Her punishment is different, though it is not hard to imagine a somewhat similar fate overtaking Maggie had she married Stephen Guest.

Isabel, however, is as free from moral conflict when she marries Osmond as Dorothea when she marries Casaubon; she thinks she is devoting herself to 'fineness'. Her story, summarised, would read: 'heiress trapped into marriage by conspirators; subsequent wretchedness.' She has been the victim of a conspiracy, like Maggie in *The Golden Bowl*, like Millie in *The Wings of the Dove*. Her innocence has been betrayed: as Strether in *The Ambassadors* is taken in by Chad and Madame de Vionnet, and as the unhappy children in *The Turn of the Screw*, *The Pupil* and *What Maisie Knew* are in one way or another victimised.

If we may make the highest comparison, George Eliot is chiefly interested in the predicament of Brutus or Macbeth, Henry James in the predicament of Hamlet, Troilus or Othello.

So completely is the lot of the two heroines reversed that one might almost imagine that it was done on purpose. Gwendolen is induced by poverty to accept Grandcourt although she sees this as a wrong done to his cast mistress and her children. Isabel is chosen by Osmond's ex-mistress, Madame Merle, to marry him – largely in the hope that her money may be helpful to her (unacknowledged) daughter Pansy.

A different fable requires a different protagonist. If Dr Leavis is right (and he probably is) in thinking that George Eliot knew her heroine better at the beginning of the book than James knew his, it was because it was more important to her at that stage. Dr Leavis also seems to find greater strength in

George Eliot's 'rendering of country-house and "county" society compared with James's'. And James himself was impressed by that strength – a strength that elsewhere he showed in an eminent degree. Here it would not have been appropriate in the American world of the Touchetts, which was only Isabel's jumping-off ground. Gwendolen had to live in the world of the Mallingers and Arrowpoints.

The suggestion (for it almost amounts to that) that Gwendolen and Isabel are the same young woman seen respectively by a woman and by a man comes perilously near to the desertion of the canons for the criticism of fiction in favour of those of biography.

'In the ladies' dining-room it was evident that Gwendolen was not a general favourite with her own sex; there were no beginnings of intimacy between her and the other girls, and in conversation they rather noted what she said than spoke to her in free exchange. Perhaps it was that she was not much interested in them, and when left alone in their company had a sense of empty benches' (ch. 11).

'James *tells* us nothing like this about Isabel,' says Dr Leavis. What can he mean by the italics if not to suggest that there is more about Isabel to know than we are told? And yet it is an elementary axiom that in fiction only the facts that we are told are facts, and only immediate and inescapable inference from them is permissible. Florence Nightingale was 'there' even when her biographers did not follow her; Gwendolen and Isabel were not.

In fact we know that Isabel, like most self-respecting people, got on better with her own sex. Henrietta Stackpoole seeks her over the world; she is a good companion (as far as anyone can be) to her very difficult aunt; Pansy, her step-daughter, is devoted to her; Miss Molyneux desires her friendship; even Madame Merle liked her before she became an heiress, even the Countess Gemini feels sympathy for her. Moreover she is charmingly sympathetic to two men who are quite out of the competition: to her invalid cousin, Ralph Touchett, and to Pansy's admirer, Edward Rosier.

Isabel was a vital young woman with strong affections for several people; there is no evidence that Gwendolen cared for anyone except (rather condescendingly) for her mother, before she fell in love with Daniel. Osmond, indeed, wished to marry Isabel for her money (and could certainly not have done so without it), but we know, and on Ralph's testimony, that he was 'greatly in love' with her. No one was greatly in love with Gwendolen – unless we count Rex Gascoigne's calf love. And yet, plunged in poverty as she is, Grandcourt wants her as an ornament. It is certain that he knows that she is aware of Mrs Glasher and her claims, and probable that he despises her in consequence.

We are also told by Dr Leavis that in Isabel Archer 'James doesn't *see* vanity or silliness', but he maintains that in such a girl there must have been expressions of 'her preoccupation with self' and her 'sense of her own absoluteness', and that 'it is hard to believe that, in life, she could be as free from qualities inviting a critical response as the Isabel Archer seen by James'. This again seems a dangerous approach towards the methods of biography.

It is, however, not the truth that we are considering the same young woman seen acutely by another woman, and almost sentimentally by a man. Isabel is a headstrong but cultivated and pleasant young woman, Gwendolen has a culture only a little superior to that of Rosamond Vincy, and is a very disagreeable young woman indeed. The 'venturesome lightness' of Gwendolen – which Dr Leavis, extraordinarily, prefers to the exquisite wit of Congreve's Millamant – associates her with the heavy playfulness of Mary Garth. George Eliot only claimed for her that 'her lively venturesomeness of talk had the effect of wit' (ch. 24). Like Mary she is 'pert as a school-girl well can be'.

It must readily be admitted that Isabel has no moral conflict, that her choice of a husband has 'neither a more intense nor a richer moral significance' than that of Gwendolen; but if James be reproached for that, it is to reproach him for not having written an entirely different book.

Gwendolen is urged forward by the pressure of poverty and the wishes of her friends. Isabel's friends, her aunt and her cousin Ralph, urge her in quite the opposite direction. It is, however, unfair to accuse her of 'unintelligent obstinacy'. Her aunt is socially ambitious, her cousin is in love with her; they are prejudiced witnesses, and neither of them had anything to object to Osmond apart from the fact that they feel his emptiness. Moreover Isabel has most carefully been led on by Madame Merle (whose secret motive is only known to Countess Gemini, who is afraid to reveal it, even if she wished to do so). Isabel's mistake is to marry an unworthy man who fascinates her, with whom she is in love, and of whom she knows no harm. Gwendolen is not in love with Grandcourt, and knows great harm of him. The reader is (in a sense) an accomplice before the fact to the marriage with Grandcourt, whom he knows (from the scenes with Lush) to be a thoroughly unpleasant character. Osmond, at worst, seems rather 'wet'; and Madame Merle's wishes for his marriage with Isabel do not appear on a first reading to go beyond quite ordinary match-making. Moreover, though great sympathy is aroused for Ralph Touchett (a far more believable and satisfying moral centre to the book than Daniel Deronda can possibly be), yet Caspar Goodwood is so boring, and Henrietta Stackpoole so irritating, that the reader is not entirely opposed to a marriage that will cause them both discomfiture; and it is a victory for Europe. Isabel has committed an error of judgment, and some imprudence may be laid to her charge; Gwendolen has done wrong (though with great provocation) and knows it.

The main characteristic of Gwendolen (which she shares with Rosamond) is a ruthless selfishness. 'Always she was the princess in exile, who in time of famine was to have her breakfast-roll made of the finest bolted flour from the seven thin ears of wheat, and in a general decampment was to have her silver fork kept out of the baggage. How was this to be accounted for? The answer may seem to lie quite on the surface – in her beauty, a certain unusualness about her, a decision of will which made itself felt in her graceful movements and clear unhesitating tones. . . But beware of arriving at conclusions without comparison. I remember having seen the same assiduous, apologetic attention awarded to persons who were not at all beautiful or unusual . . . Some of them were a very common sort of men. And the only point of resemblance among them all was a strong determination to have what was pleasant, with a total fearlessness in making themselves disagreeable or dangerous when they did not get it' (ch. 4). She is also akin to Tito, who at all costs would avoid what was unpleasant to him. Isabel's effect on the world around her is quite different – her sister, her brother-in-law, her aunt, her cousin are all in some way critical. We are not shown her marriage until it has lasted some years, and we never want to say 'serve her right': the Grandcourt marriage is a union of two 'torpedoes', and the colder wins. Not for a moment have we expected it to be happy. There are moments when we are inclined to feel – not wholly without satisfaction – that Lydgate has been avenged.

We are surprised that intelligent men should have so much faith in Gwendolen's (ultimate) worth. Klesmer tells her: "I should require your words to be what your face and form are – always among the meanings of a noble music" (ch. 11). This is to require much – but we saw that George Eliot thought the effect of poor Hetty's prettiness analogous to that of exquisite music. Nevertheless it is hard to think of Gwendolen as 'a grand sweet song'. If she ever gets to the degree of 'a melody that's sweetly played in tune' – which can be predicated of Isabel – she will have done well enough.

She is an illustration of George Eliot's version of the doctrine that 'sin is behovely'. Before he has any certainty about her past Daniel says: "Those who would be comparatively uninteresting beforehand may become worthier of sympathy when they do something that awakens in them keen remorse. Lives are enlarged in different ways. I daresay some would never get their eyes opened if it were not from a violent shock from the consequences of their own actions" (ch. 36). Later, when he knows a little more, he says: "One who has committed irremediable errors may be scourged by that consciousness into a higher course than is common." He encourages Gwendolen to think that she may live "to be one of the best of women, who make others glad that they were born". She cannot see how this will come to pass, nor can we.

'Osmond so plainly *is* Grandcourt, hardly disguised, that the general derivative relation of James's novel to George Eliot's becomes quite unquestionable': thus writes Dr Leavis.

Their external position is very different. Grandcourt is almost certain to inherit a baronetcy, and likely to come into a peerage; he has two estates of his own, and two more in reversion. He has therefore an unassailable social position, and is certain of preeminence whatever his personal endowments may be. Physically and in manner 'he is not ridiculous' – so says Gwendolen, whose standards are high. It is true that his uncle thinks him 'a pale-blooded mortal' and Vandernoodt finds him 'a washed-out piece of cambric'. He has a great tendency to be bored, except when on horseback.

Towards the world Grandcourt is generally misanthropic: 'His mind was much furnished with a sense of what brutes his fellow-creatures were, both masculine and feminine; what odious familiarities they had, what smirks, what modes of flourishing their handkerchiefs, what costume, what lavender water, what bulging eyes, and what foolish notions of making themselves agreeable by remarks which were not wanted.' Nevertheless he depended (as did Gwendolen) on a 'world of admiring or envying spectators'.

Osmond, unlike Grandcourt, has no social position and not much money; he is an expatriate American brought in youth with his sister to Europe by their mother, the 'American Corinne'. As a physical type he is very unlike: 'His dense, delicate hair, his overdrawn, retouched features, his clear complexion, ripe without being coarse, the very evenness of the growth of his beard, and that light, smooth slenderness of structure which made the movement of a single one of his fingers produce the effect of an expressive gesture – these personal points struck our sensitive young woman as signs of quality, of intensity, somehow as promises of interest.'[6] It is true that the hypersensitivity of a potentially fine nature may come to resemble, in action, the irritability of a nature fundamentally coarse: perhaps this is the true contrast and likeness between the two Osmonds and the two Grandcourts.

We are told (by Dr Leavis) that 'Osmond's interest in articles of *virtù* amounts to nothing more than a notation of a kind of cherished fastidiousness of conscious, but empty, superiority that is precisely Grandcourt's'.

We are never quite sure of Osmond's taste. Rosier did not think much of it, and the first glimpse of the villa on the Florentine hill-top is not very attractive: 'a variety of those faded hangings of damask and tapestry, those chests and

[6] *Portrait of a Lady*, ch. 24.

cabinets of carved and time-polished oak, those angular specimens of pictorial art in frames as pedantically primitive, those perverse-looking relics of mediaeval brass and pottery, of which Italy has long been the not quite exhausted store-house.' Madame Merle, however, looking 'at the old cabinets, pictures, tapestries, surfaces of faded silk', speaks of Osmond's 'adorable taste'. She might be speaking of an entirely different room. She has so much been built up in our minds as an *arbiter elegantiarum* that we are inclined to admit Osmond, on her testimonial, to the company of Mr and Mrs Gereth, those devoted collectors who with little money and much patience created an interior that was a real artistic achievement.[7] It was as such that he first appealed to Isabel.

That such an appeal, so largely aesthetic (though it must involve other values as well) should not touch Dr Leavis is not surprising. He seems unable to feel the Paris of Gloriani's garden, that Strether in *The Ambassadors* perceives to have been such a lack in his previous life. He is unable to believe J. M. Keynes that the beautiful Cambridge of his time could excite the envy of an outside visitor like D. H. Lawrence.

Nevertheless in Osmond's garden, with its magnificent view, a serpent was lurking that was not in Gloriani's garden nor the gardens of Cambridge. Osmond was pining for appreciation. He was, it appears, a man who made a point of striving for nothing, and seeking for nothing, and retiring to a hill-top to wait for everyone and everything to come to him. Some such people wait for ever, and Osmond had already waited a little too long before Madame Merle brought Isabel into his web. He was embittered, as Grandcourt never was, for he had never known neglect. In consequence, though he had qualities that Grandcourt lacked, he was more feline and spiteful. The fact that Grandcourt's self-satisfaction depended in part on envious spectators of his position could not be really important so long as he never lacked them.

While Isabel and Osmond had started their life together in mutual love, Grandcourt and Gwendolen began with very different feelings. Grandcourt (correctly) 'believed that this girl was rather exceptional in the fact that, in spite of his

[7] We may remember that James's visual taste was probably no better than George Eliot's.

assiduous attention to her, she was not in love with him, and it seemed to him very likely that if it had not been for the sudden poverty which had come over her family, she would not have accepted him . . . On the whole Grandcourt got more pleasure out of this notion than he could have done out of winning a girl of whom he was sure that she had a strong inclination for him personally' (ch. 27). George Eliot, indeed, uses the word 'enamoured' about him, but we can probably translate this as desire for the physical possession of a handsome woman, who would make a suitable impression now as Mrs Grandcourt, and later as Lady Mallinger. There would also be an element of sadism: we know that Grandcourt, who was 'reputed' to love dogs (ch. 12), delighted in provoking their jealousy.

Gwendolen, as we have seen, approached marriage with well-founded scruples of conscience about Lydia Glasher, but none about herself as a future wife. 'It was characteristic that, with all her debating, she was never troubled by the question whether the indefensibleness of her marriage did not include the fact that she had accepted Grandcourt solely as a man whom it was convenient for her to marry, not in the least as one to whom she would be binding herself in duty' (ch. 29). She had no compunction about selling herself, and giving the buyer a bad bargain; and she evidently expected and intended to have her own way after marriage.

On her wedding day she received the family diamonds with Mrs Glasher's note: "The man you have married has a withered heart . . . I am the grave in which your chance of happiness is buried as well as mine" (ch. 31). Grandcourt entered upon a melodramatic scene: Gwendolen was pallid and shrieking, with the jewels scattered round her on the floor.

After a honeymoon at Ryelands, Grandcourt and Gwendolen went to stay with Sir Hugo Mallinger at Topping Abbey. 'Already, in seven short weeks, which seemed half her life, her husband had gained a mastery which she could no more resist than she could have resisted the benumbing effect from the touch of a torpedo.' And with a will as ineluctable as the instinct of a crab or a boa-constrictor, Grandcourt combines an acute perception of Gwendolen's weak points. "He delights in making the dogs and horses quail: that is half his pleasure in calling them his," she says to herself; ". . . It will come so to me;

and I shall quail. What else is there for me? I will not say to the
world, 'Pity me' " (ch. 35).

He will find every way to be offensive – he will attack her for
the "vulgarity" of having a secret with Daniel about the
turquoise necklace (he is too indifferent, too much self-satisfied
to feel jealousy); he will impose his factotum Lush upon
Gwendolen, although before marriage he had promised not to
do so; he will drag her off upon a yachting cruise, with only
himself for company. We are not told that he has come to hate
his wife, but this is an inescapable inference; only hatred could
make him so acute, so clever at designing ways of giving her
pain.

Osmond is not quite the same. In the great Chapter 42 we
are told of his 'faculty for making everything wither that he
touched', but 'the house of darkness, the house of dumbness,
the house of suffocation' where Isabel finds herself reminds one
more of Casaubon. 'Osmond's beautiful mind gave it neither
light nor air.' Like Dorothea, Isabel has deceived herself
with the idea of a beautiful mind; there is no evidence of
Grandcourt having any mind at all, or that anyone at any time
thought so. The 'aesthetic' and the 'sporting' exteriors of
Osmond and Grandcourt must bear some relation to some
internal difference between them. Moreover, as well as on
articles of *virtù*, Osmond was an authority on Metastasio.

We are given no glimpse of Isabel's married life until it has
gone on for some four years. She has borne and lost a child, and
has apparently got over it: it would seem that the collapse of
her happiness with Osmond has not been quite immediate.
Unlike Gwendolen, she could escape: Gwendolen has no
money, and will ruin her mother as well as herself if she leaves
Grandcourt; Isabel could easily detach herself – her aunt has
given her the example – but she is held to her place by affection
for her step-daughter, Pansy. This affection gives Osmond
subtle opportunities of hurting her (and subtle they have to be,
as he wishes to be adored by his daughter) and gives Isabel a
tragic position that the self-centred Gwendolen lacks. Moreover a conflict of affections (and therefore of duties) is caused
by Osmond's jealousy of her fraternal relations with her
cousin Ralph – a jealousy that seems to proceed partly from a
dislike of her possessing any friend of her own – and in especial

one likely to criticise him and to sustain her in any possible rebellion. It proceeds also from a pure wish to give pain – and even more from the hostility of a mean and petty nature for one so generous, with a 'daily beauty in his life'.

Even if we admit in Isabel a little pig-headedness in her original choice of Osmond, this will be no more than the 'fatal flaw' which is the cause of a tragedy altogether beyond her deserving. She grows to her full moral height before the end of the book.

Gwendolen has done a real wrong, her sufferings are a punishment, and her position has nothing of the tragic in it – except that by the punishment she is to be purged and ennobled.

Each of these heroines has a confidant or confessor, and here again the roles are reversed. Isabel's confidant is her cousin Ralph, whom she loves as if he were her brother, and who is in love with her. Gwendolen, on the other hand, has as her adviser Daniel Deronda, with whom she is in love, but whose affections are engaged elsewhere. It is only when Ralph is on his death-bed that Isabel fully admits her mistake to him. He has, indeed some feeling of guilt towards her: "I always understood . . . though it was so strange – so pitiful. You wanted to look at life for yourself – but you were not allowed, you were punished for your wish. You were ground in the very mill of the conventional."[8] But it was he who had persuaded his father to leave her the means to carry out that wish. "I don't believe that such a generous mistake as yours can hurt you for more than a little," he tells her.

Gwendolen, on the other hand, has made an ungenerous mistake, and from the first feels compunction towards Daniel. He has heard the story of Lydia Glasher from Vandernoodt, a guest at Topping Abbey, and it filled his mind with conjecture.

'Since the early days when he tried to construct the hidden story of his own birth, his mind had perhaps never been so active in weaving probabilities about any private affair as it had now begun to be about Gwendolen's marriage. This unavowed relation of Grandcourt's – could she have gained some knowledge of it, which caused her to shrink from the

[8] *Portrait of a Lady*, ch. 54.

match – a shrinking finally overcome by the urgence of poverty? He could recall almost every word she had said to him, and in certain of these words he seemed to discern that she was conscious of having done some wrong – inflicted some injury. His own acute experience made him alive to the form of injury which might affect the unavowed children and their mother. Was Mrs Grandcourt, under all her determined show of satisfaction, gnawed by a double, a treble-headed grief – self-reproach, disappointment, jealousy? . . . He thought he saw clearly enough now why Sir Hugo had never dropped any hint of this affair to him; and immediately the image of this Mrs Glasher became painfully associated with his own hidden birth. Gwendolen knowing of that woman and her children, marrying Grandcourt and showing herself contented, would have been among the most repulsive of beings to him; but Gwendolen tasting the bitterness of remorse for having contributed to their injury was brought very near to his fellow-feeling' (ch. 37). This motivation of Daniel's is a particularly able construction – strong enough to support his subsequent relation as lay-confessor to Gwendolen, if he were were less heavily pompous in it.

Mutatis mutandis Daniel's charity towards Gwendolen is reminiscent of that of Caleb Garth towards Bulstrode – though it contains more hope. "That is the heaviest of all – to wear the yoke of our own wrong-doing. But if you submitted to that as men submit to maiming or life-long incurable disease? – and made the unalterable wrong a reason for more effort toward a good, that may do something to counterbalance the evil? One who has committed irremediable errors may be scourged by that consciousness into a higher course than is common. There are many examples. Feeling what it is to have spoiled one life may well make us long to save other lives from being spoiled" (ch. 36). This is his best moment with her.

George Eliot repeats another theme, that of the would-be murderer who is not quite a murderer. Caterina had taken up a dagger, but found Wybrow dead of heart-failure through no action of hers. Hetty Sorrel abandoned her baby, and went back too late to retrieve it. Bulstrode gave Raffles the brandy that he hoped and believed would kill him, though most practitioners would have prescribed it. Gwendolen is another variation on the theme – a journalist who lately described her as a 'hysteric with murderous impulses' was much overstating the case against her. Her inaction may, improbably, have caused Grandcourt's death – which she greatly desired – but she cannot tell if, or how much it was willed.

Like Caterina, she had at one time armed herself with a dagger, 'small and sharp like a long willow leaf in a silver sheath'. She locked it into the drawer in her dressing-case, but threw the key into the sea when she was on the yacht. It is perhaps significant that she did not throw the dagger.

In a sudden gust, Grandcourt fell into the water. " 'The rope!' he called out in a voice – not his own – I hear it now – and I stooped for the rope – I felt I must – . . . That was in my mind – he would come back. But he was gone down again, and I had the rope in my hand – I don't know what I thought – I was leaping away from myself – I would have saved him then. I was leaping from my crime, and there it was – close to me as I fell – there was the dead face – dead, dead" (ch. 56).

The 'dead face', an improbable and awkward symbol – that would be more in place in a 'gothic' novel – had first been seen on a panel of the wainscot at Offendene: 'an upturned dead face, from which an obscure figure seemed to be fleeing with outstretched arms' (ch. 3). We are offered no explanation of the existence of this oddity at Offendene, a conventional small, country house, apparently the dower house of Lord Brackenshaw's family. The panel was opened by Gwendolen's small half-sister, Isabel, and then promptly locked at Gwendolen's orders. In the tableau enacted in the Christmas vacation, with Gwendolen as Hermione, the panel flew open again at the vibration of a 'thunderous chord' struck by Klesmer on the piano – Isabel had unlocked it for another glimpse (ch. 6).

The image continues to haunt her. When she begins to desire Grandcourt's death: "I saw his dead face . . . ever so long ago I saw it and I wished him to be dead" (ch. 56). After he has been drowned she says: "His face will not be seen above the water again. . . Not by anyone else – only by me – a dead face – I shall never get away from it." And, later: "If he were here again, what should I do? I cannot wish him here – and yet I cannot bear his dead face. . . Sometimes I thought he would kill *me* if I resisted his will. But now – his dead face is there, and I cannot bear it."

Deronda is her lay confessor, and, on the whole, gives her the sound advice that her author would no doubt have given her; though he is sententious, and is less merciful than Gilfil is to Caterina. It is true that the circumstances are not identical. Wybrow unquestionably died without any activity on Caterina's part, whatever she might have intended. There cannot be the same absolute certainty that prompt action on Gwendolen's part might not have saved Grandcourt. Nevertheless, it is not the consequences that should weigh most heavily with the confessor. Gwendolen's evil will is a momentary impulse, promptly repented – Caterina on the other hand has formed a murderous plan, even though we may feel it improbable that she could have carried it out had it come to the point. Moreover, a sin of omission is so much easier to commit: easier to refrain from throwing a rope than to plunge a dagger into the heart.

It is the falsest of all commonplaces that we are all capable of murder, a crime which demands a colossal vanity on the part of the murderer, and a feeling that his convenience is of more importance than another's life. No character of George Eliot's is capable of murder by commission: Caterina would not have carried her 'malice aforethought' into action; Hetty hoped that her baby might be saved; Bulstrode's casuistry left loopholes for excuse. But homicide by omission, as the result of an instantaneous reaction, might be anyone's crime, and Gwendolen has the reader's pardon, in so far as she needs it. She will be doomed to a perpetual uncertainty about what she has really done. What she has been guilty of is the sin of Godfrey Cass and of Mrs Transome – hatred, and the desire of another's death. In this case George Eliot has shown to what it may lead, and has given *ex post facto* justification to her severity towards those characters.

We understand from Klesmer and from Daniel Deronda (who, prig and bore though he is, does convince us that he has spiritual insight) that Gwendolen is a great soul and that she is called to a life of extreme goodness. There are hints that the supernatural virtues will not be excluded: "The refuge you are needing from personal trouble is the higher, the religious life, which builds an enthusiasm for something more than our own appetites and interests" (ch. 36). So Mauriac tells us that his Thérèse Desqueyroux is called to sanctity. We have to take this on faith – but in Gwendolen's story there is something like an epitome of George Eliot's most characteristic moral teaching. We see her fall into temptation, and yield to it (like Arthur, like Maggie); we see her cherish thoughts of hatred and wish for another's death (like Caterina, like Godfrey Cass, like Mrs Transome, like Bulstrode) and we see her terribly punished for it by being doomed to a perpetual doubt whether her inactivity has caused Grandcourt's death. We see her, raised by remorse, from somewhere below the level of the *honnêtes gens* to the level of the morally elect – at least we are aware that that is her destiny. She is the only one of George Eliot's heroines who is thus left rising in the right direction – for Dorothea slightly came down, and Maggie died. (One does not count Romola, who remains, as she always was, enskyed and sainted.)

The deplorable Zionist activities of Daniel Deronda – which history has rendered ridiculous as an intended contribution to world peace – show how wise George Eliot had been in her early resolution to be 'the *aesthetic*, not the doctrinal teacher', how right to be opposed to 'the prescribing of special measures, concerning which the artistic mind, however moved by social sympathy, is often not the best judge'. This part of the book is an object lesson for would-be political novelists.

IX   Conclusion

It is not only in *Middlemarch*, though that is her greatest triumph in that sort, that George Eliot has set people firmly in their social background, and generally in their work or property. Sometimes she has been overpraised for her knowledge of men's lives: we have seen that Casaubon is convincing as a writer, but not entirely as a scholar, and that we can believe in Lydgate as a practitioner, though not as a scientist. In the same way, though we can accept Klesmer's serious devotion to his art, we believe in him as an executant, but not at all as a composer. Of the important male characters, only Daniel Deronda, Felix Holt and Ladislaw are not securely tethered to the world immediately around them, and each of them is almost universally considered a failure. Their activities as public men are not clearly and distinctly envisaged. Ladislaw, 'working well in those times when reforms were begun with a young hopefulness of immediate good which has been much checked in our days', is vague enough; Felix Holt can hardly find full employment in his library for working men. In her own day, when 'hopefulness of immediate good' had grown grey hairs, she had only an absurd eastern adventure as a way of disposing of Daniel Deronda.

'There is no private life which has not been determined by a wider public life, from the time when the primeval milkmaid had to wander with the wanderings of her clan, because the cow she milked was one of a herd which had made the pastures bare.' But the word 'determined' is too strong, and so her fables show us. 'Enthusiasm', indeed, is for economic reasons more prevalent in Stonyshire and in the world of Lantern Yard than in Hayslope or Raveloe, where the Napoleonic wars have enriched the farmers. But the farmers' prosperity is only a background to the stories of Adam Bede, the carpenter, or Silas Marner, the weaver. The events before and after the

Reform Bill of 1832 have a great effect on the inhabitants of Middlemarch and Treby, but they do not really touch the lives of Dorothea and Casaubon, of Rosamond and Lydgate, of Bulstrode, of Mary Garth and Fred Vincy, of Jermyn and Mrs Transome. George Eliot has been overpraised for her social and economic thinking, but it is often irrelevant to her novels – as for example the famous passage in *The Mill on the Floss* about the costliness of 'good society', when at St Ogg's there is neither 'good society', nor those who pay for it.

Nevertheless, the solidity of the setting, in spite of its occasional irrelevance, does give authenticity to the stories; we should probably feel its lack in *Daniel Deronda* even if George Eliot had not there broken her wise resolution against 'the prescribing of special measures'. And though, on the whole, we can endorse Henry James's praise of her 'county' life, we may feel some doubts about the roving archery meeting, and about Gwendolen's performance as Hermione.

George Eliot is more impressive as an ethical writer. A novelist should probably not aspire to be a teacher but is likely (whether responsibly or not – and this author is always responsible) to exhibit a moral point-of-view, to prefer some virtues and to have an especial detestation for some vices. In order not to confuse the issue by speaking of 'Christian' morality, one may say that any significant writer will have behind him 'traditional' or Aristotelian morality, however he may interpret it. As Ivy Compton-Burnett said: 'You must recognise certain moral laws. Otherwise you couldn't have any human life, any literature or anything.' This is the essential humanist standpoint, and literature (if so it may be called) which denies or ignores the existence of moral laws is doomed to a life that will be nasty, brutish and short.

This does not mean that a writer's ethics must be purely conventional. Ivy Compton-Burnett, a severe moralist of the late Victorian agnostic school, had a very decided position of her own: liberal views about sex, a passionate hatred of abuse of power, great tolerance of human weakness, and merciless loathing of 'ugly behaviour'. Nor do all those writers who largely derive their philosophy from G. E. Moore's *Principia Ethica* have an identical point-of-view. They all believe in the supreme value of good states of being, and of personal relations;

but E. M. Forster added some heresies of his own, which I
have elsewhere tried to expose.[1]

George Eliot cannot be said to teach by example. Her most
likeable good characters are generally to be ranked among the
honnêtes gens, and she often apologises for them: such are
Maynard Gilfil, Adolphus Irwine, Dolly Winthrop, Nancy
Lammeter, Lucy Deane, Philip Wakem, Celia Chettam,
Sir Hugo Mallinger and Henry Gascoigne. The stumbling
Maggie and the less exalted sides of Dorothea demand sympathy,
while Romola leaves us cold. The more 'perfect' characters
seek perfection as evangelicals or methodists, as *Piagnoni*, as
radicals, as Jews of the strict observance – in short, in worlds
dreadfully lacking in 'sweetness and light'. Nevertheless
perfection can be sought – e.g. by Quakers, Anglo-Catholics
and (possibly) Christian Scientists, without any sacrifice of
'sweetness and light', which seem so incompatible with dissent.

The heroes do not form an impressive portrait gallery,
though sympathy may be felt for the honest worth of Adam, of
Silas or of Caleb, for the well-meaning Fred Vincy, the
crushed Lydgate and the morally improved Arthur Donnithorne and Godfrey Cass. Virginia Woolf felt that the failure
over Philip Wakem and Stephen Guest was due to George
Eliot's despair of creating a mate worthy of the noble Maggie.
Of the heroines she said they 'bring out the worst in her, lead
her into difficult places, make her self-conscious, didactic, and
occasionally vulgar'. She almost wished to 'delete the whole
sisterhood'. Had she done so – for there would be even less
reason to spare the heroes – we should be left, indeed, with an
admirable world of farmers and their wives, carpenters,
lawyers, auctioneers and clergymen; but the effect of any one
of the novels is in the whole, not in the parts, and none of them
can be read like a Waverley novel, with almost total disregard
of the central theme and the interest confined to the background and minor characters.

It is in the whole of each book that her teaching lies, in the
slow development of effects, and in the unrolling of the
consequence of actions. Her examples do not greatly edify us,
nor is her own personality or her individual voice important.

---

[1] *A Treatise on the Novel* (London 1947), pp. 64–70.

We never feel inclined to examine our consciences in the light of her moral sense – as we may do with profit in the light shed by Jane Austen or Ivy Compton-Burnett. It would be a serious thing to earn the disapproval of either of those two writers, whereas one would care little for that of George Eliot. We do not love her, and – though it is certain that people did so – it is now hard to imagine it.

What she has to teach is a method. It was and is a useful thing to re-establish casuistry, and to insist on the double standard. Everyone who has principles other than those of the *honnêtes gens* – whether as Christian, communist, pacifist, vegetarian, etc. – will sometimes require the help of the casuist if he is to live among the *honnêtes gens* without hypocrisy or loss of ideals. Even the *honnêtes gens* themselves may have need of casuistry when circumstances create for them what looks like a conflict of duties. There are, of course, people who boast of having a standard they can live up to – for example, the rule never to do deliberate harm to another human creature. But the lowness of such a standard must be evident if we imagine anyone admitting that he did not accept that rule – he would not be a moral agent at all. Moreover, conduct is always lower than the standard aimed at. If the casuist can preserve standards, put in danger by puritan intransigence, he does well.

George Eliot herself was, no doubt, obliged to make use of casuistry in her own case. She may have believed in Truthfulness, but her anonymity involved her in a tissue of falsehood. This is not to say that she was not justified in this, or in her rejection of Chastity (in which she also, no doubt, believed). She could have had no religious scruples about joining Lewes as his wife, for she was no longer a believer; there was no human impediment, for Agnes Lewes had no claim upon him. She may, however, have felt some hesitation about her right to defy society – and there certainly were unbelievers who questioned that right. 'No one whom I have heard speak, speaks in other than terms of respect of Mrs Lewes,' wrote Charles Eliot Norton,[2] 'but the common feeling is that it will not do for society to condone so flagrant a breach as hers of a

_____
[2] cit. Haight *Letters*, v, p. 7.

convention and a sentiment (to use no stronger terms) on which morality greatly relies for support. I suspect society is right in this.' Being for a time on the defensive, she had all the keener interest in the problems of a Maggie or a Romola.

John Holloway[3] calls attention to her limited cast. No character of hers is brutally selfish (perhaps he makes too much allowance for Rosamond, for Grandcourt and for the early Gwendolen). Only Baldassare and Mr Tulliver know real hatred; only Stephen Guest approaches physical passion. 'No one is savage, no one is depraved. The world of serious characters divides into the good and the weak.' The people, worked on by each other, or by their own past, sink into evil or folly by slow degrees, or mount slowly to better things – and it is in the unfolding of these slow processes that the great success of these novels lies.

Nevertheless much is excluded from her picture of life that especially delights in other English novels. Her most disagreeable people are cold 'torpedoes'; there are few speeches with second intentions, few flashes of malice or brilliant counterstrokes against it. Moreover the solid setting of the characters and their interwoven lives is not without its disadvantages; it makes it almost impossible for her to add to the gallery of the great eccentrics of English literature. The 'Dickens character' is nearly always self-employed or unemployable, and is frequently *sans famille*.

Her literary reputation has fluctuated. Overestimated in her life-time, it was considerably deflated by Leslie Stephen. Meredith had assisted in the depreciation by his phrase about 'the mercurial little showman and the errant woman'. Edmund Gosse had seen her as a 'large, thickset sibyl, dreamy and immobile, whose massive features, somewhat grim when seen in profile, were incongruously bordered by a hat, always in the height of Paris fashion, which in those days commonly included an immense ostrich feather – this was George Eliot. The contrast between the solemnity of the face and the frivolity of the headgear had something pathetic and provincial about it.' Thus she appears in a pencil sketch made by Lady Alma-Tadema in the author's fifty-eighth year. Those people who

---

[3] *The Victorian Sage* (London 1953), pp. 121f.

had had the privilege of invitations to the Priory were inclined to be facetious about their recollections – remembered words seemed droll, and they were apt to giggle over the picture of one earnest young woman or another on her knees before the sibyl, with her head in the black satin lap.

Nevertheless, *Middlemarch* never lost its hold. Mrs Cornish started to re-read it on her death-bed. Virginia Woolf could write of it as 'one of the few English novels written for grown-up people'. Yet, herself a more delicate stylist, she was justifiably hard on George Eliot's writing: 'Her hold on dialogue, when it is not dialect, is slack . . . she allows her heroines to talk too much. She has little verbal felicity.' The subsequent revaluation of George Eliot has gone too far – and when we are asked to admire the 'archness' of Mary Garth or the 'venturesome lightness' of Gwendolen Harleth more than the brilliance of Millamant, we can be very sure that the author's reputation is due for another slump.

One of the aims of this book is a protective and partial depreciation – a jettisoning of false and exaggerated claims, and an admission of weaknesses. It is hoped that the resultant image of George Eliot, though unflattered, may yet be seen worthy of deep respect – a respect that may be more readily given when worship is not required and love is not expected.

For though a most imperfect artist, she is a great novelist, and though we deny her our affection, she commands our admiration – and that largely for reasons that defy definition. Critics as far apart as Virginia Woolf and Dr Leavis agree that her world is *there*. Hayslope, Raveloe, Shepperton and Middlemarch are *there* as much as Jane Austen's Highbury – though Florence is not there at all. And her characters are there, even when they are tiresome – apart from Ladislaw, Felix and Daniel. Yet it is probably only her greatest book, *Middlemarch*, that anyone now opens with expectation of unclouded pleasure, and closes with unmixed regret.

Index

Titles of works by George Eliot are printed in capitals. The names of characters or fictitious places from the novels are printed in italics.